Better safe than sorry. We have taken the utmost care to verify our facts, but opening hours can change at short notice, or a bar may be fully booked or closed during your perfect weekend in Berlin. We highly recommend that you make reservations as early as possible before your trip – a simple phone call is all that is required to confirm your date and favourite venue.

© 2015 Süddeutsche Zeitung GmbH, Munich
for the Süddeutsche Zeitung Edition
in cooperation with smart-travelling print UG, Berlin
Series 'A perfect weekend ...'

Idea and concept: Nicola Bramigk, Nancy Bachmann
Project management: Till Brömer, Sabine Sternagel, Jasmin Seitner
Texts: Nancy Bachmann, Sabine Danek, Karolin Langfeldt
Photos: Nicola Bramigk, Soho House pp. 18-21, Design Hotels pp. 16-17,
Linnen Berlin p. 23, Harry Weber pp. 24-25, Mani Hotel p. 22
Cover design: Stefan Dimitrov, Lena Mahr
Layout and illustration: Cindy Bachmann, Verena Bettin
City map: Verena Bettin
Prepress: Daniela Mecklenburg
Production: Thekla Licht, Hermann Weixler
Print and binding: optimal media GmbH, Röbel/Müritz
ISBN: 978-3-86497-333-8

1st English edition (based on 11th revised German edition)

SMART TRAVELLING

A PERFECT WEEKEND ...
BERLIN

www.smart-travelling.net

BERLIN'S TOP LOCATIONS

Hotel: 25hours Hotel Bikini Berlin
Budapester Straße 40, Charlottenburg
Phone: 0049 (0)30 1202210
Page 9

Hotel: Soho House Hotel
Torstraße 1, Mitte
Phone: 0049 (0)30 4050440
Page 19

Restaurant: Lokal
Linienstraße 160, Mitte
Phone: 0049 (0)30 28449500
Page 27

Restaurant: Sale e Tabacchi
Rudi-Dutschke-Straße 18, Kreuzberg
Phone: 0049 (0)30 2521155
Page 37

Restaurant: Grill Royal
Friedrichstraße 105 b, Mitte
Phone: 0049 (0)30 28879288
Page 47

Restaurant: Cookies Cream
Behrenstraße 55, Mitte
Phone: 0049 (0)30 27492940
Page 55

☞ Further tips can be found at www.smart-travelling.net

Restaurant: eins44 Kantine
Elbestraße 28/29, Neukölln
Phone: 0049 (0)30 62981212
Page 59

Restaurant: Paris Bar
Kantstraße 152, Charlottenburg
Phone: 0049 (0)30 3138052
Page 65

Café: The Barn Roastery
Schönhauser Allee 8,
Prenzlauer Berg
Page 73

Bar: Victoria Bar
Potsdamer Straße 102, Tiergarten
Phone: 0049 (0)30 25759977
Page 79

Shop: Markthalle Neun
Eisenbahnstraße 42/43, Kreuzberg
Phone: 0049 (0)30 61073473
Page 85

Miscellaneous
Tips, excursions and walking tours
Page 89

WONDERFUL, WONDERFUL BERLIN!

The most enthralling city in the West, Europe's New York, a young person's paradise – to mention just a few of the town's many accolades. The sky is the limit when it comes to superlatives about Berlin. The city's magical allure permanently entices visitors from around the world whether it's for a weekend break, a few months or an entire lifetime. Many regard Germany's capital as a place of limitless opportunities. Opening a nightclub or restaurant, starting a new business or realizing an art project all seem like easy ventures here. The metropolis with its 3.5-million population offers enough space to live and dream. Every week new restaurants open in Neukölln's secluded courtyards or bars appear on the roofs of car parks; in Charlottenburg innovative stores and galleries open their doors, while in Kreuzberg, after the street food market, the latest craze is the breakfast club. Berlin Mitte is also the heartland for Michelin-starred chefs and trendy clubs.

Berlin's cool venues are as much a talking point as its architectural gems and historic attractions that have delighted visitors for centuries and in recent decades: the Museum Island, Tiergarten, the Neue Nationalgalerie, the Jewish Museum or the Berlin Wall Memorial. Berlin is a hive of activity where it's best to follow your passions. Wander in and out of the galleries and museums, explore the local bars, enjoy a leisurely brunch or relax and unwind in Tiergarten park surrounded by large Turkish families enjoying barbecue feasts.

Hotel Restaurant Café Bar Shop // Interview Interesting facts Recipe

25HOURS HOTEL BIKINI BERLIN

At the latest since the 25hours Hotel opened in Berlin's City West district it's clear that this part of the city is alive and kicking. For a long while the East's hip districts like Berlin Mitte and Prenzlauer Berg captivated the trendsetters and tourists. Yet, things changed during 2014. Adjacent to the hotel are the famous gallery C|O Berlin, the avant-garde Bikini shopping mall and the irresistible Paris Bar. The 25hours hotel is the perfect base for exploring this new terrain, and avoiding the more familiar and busier tourist trails. The 149 rooms feature modern and urban interiors that are the signature style of the twenty-five hours hotel chain. Guest accommodation is on the fourth to ninth floors: half of the rooms have fabulous views over Berlin Zoo, while the other half overlooks the western cityscape. Frequent travellers who previously stayed in the East will be pleasantly surprised by the panoramic views of the metropolis from this high-rise building. The 25hours may not fulfil all the criteria of a star-rated hotel such as room service, but the city traveller will appreciate more valuable amenities like free Wifi, free MINI car hire and rent-a-bike – ideal for cycling through the adjacent park.

25hours Hotel Bikini Berlin Address: Budapester Straße 40, Charlottenburg
Phone: 0049 (0)30 1202210 Website: www.25hours-hotels.com
Price: Double from €105

-11-

Hotel Restaurant Café Bar Shop // Interview Interesting facts Recipe

☞ Monkey Bar

Monkey Bar is Berlin's hottest new venue. It is located on the tenth floor of the 25hours hotel. Here you can sip a Moscow Mule and watch the monkeys opposite in Berlin's Zoo. Unfortunately, you can expect to wait at peak times when the bar gets crowded, but hotel guests have priority entry privileges. Drinks cost more than the average for Berlin and although the quality is fairly mediocre, the views and sunny terrace more than make up for it.

Address: Budapester Straße 40, Phone: 0049 (0)30 120221210
Opening hours: Sunday – Thursday noon – 1 a.m. and
Friday – Saturday noon – 2 a.m.

Hotel Restaurant Café Bar Shop // Interview Interesting facts Recipe

☞ Neni Restaurant

The Neni Restaurant, which belongs to the 25hours hotels, adopts the same concept in every city: it's all about dining together and sharing. The best idea is to order different dishes for everyone to try like curry houmous with pan-fried king prawns, Pastrami sandwiches, baba ganoush or salmon marinated in oriental spices. The menu is an eclectic mix of Persian, Russian, Arabic, Moroccan, Turkish, Spanish, German and Austrian influences.

Address: Budapester Straße 40, Phone: 0049 (0)30 120221200
Opening hours: Monday – Friday noon – 11 p.m. and
Saturday – Sunday 12:30 p.m. – 11 p.m.

👉 Hotel Zoo

The West has another newcomer, although strictly speaking Hotel Zoo is one of Berlin's historic greats. At one time or another, Romy Schneider, Grace Kelly and Erich Kästner all stayed in this building, which dates back to the 19th century. Having faded into the background for years, the hotel was re-opened in autumn 2014. Exposed brick walls, high ceilings with hand-finished stucco details and industrial-size expansive windows create a distinctive ambiance. Each of the 130 guest rooms and 15 suites is unique, although all are decorated with a blend of industrial elegance combined with parquet flooring, leather, velvet and exotic design details.

Address: Kurfürstendamm 25, 10719 Berlin, Phone: 0049 (0)30 884370
Website: www.hotelzoo.de, Price: Double from €120

Hotel   Restaurant   Café   Bar   Shop   //   Interview   Interesting facts   Recipe

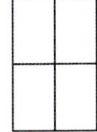

SOHO HOUSE HOTEL

The idea of a modern 'gentlemen's club' for people with creative careers was launched in 1995 in London's trendy Soho district. Exclusive, but relaxed – the concept of the founder Nick Jones proved popular and sister hotels soon opened in New York und Hollywood. Since May 2010 Berlin's artists and creative people have been able to enjoy an alternative living space for networking, private parties, work and the spa – all for a monthly members' subscription that costs little more than joining a gym. This late Bauhaus style listed building is steeped in history: it opened in the 1930s as a department store, later becoming the seat of the Communist Party's Central Committee and the first president of the GDR. Today's modern building reflects the zeitgeist with an easy blend of English luxury and industrial chic.

If you're lucky enough to check into one of the 40 stylish rooms – from 'tiny' to 'extra large' – there's no real reason to leave Soho House. Hotel guests are also club members for the duration of their stay. That means relaxing in the lounge in plush armchairs by the fireside, pampering in the spa with its exclusive Cowshed products or visiting the rooftop bar and pool and admiring the unique view of Alexanderplatz and the TV tower. There's no better, or more relaxing place to stay in Berlin Mitte!

Soho House Hotel   Address: Torstraße 1, Mitte
Phone: 0049 (0)30 4050440   Website: www.sohohouseberlin.com
Price: Double from €110

Hotel Restaurant Café Bar Shop // Interview Interesting facts Recipe

☞ Mani Hotel

The Mani is located amid the hustle and bustle of Rosenthaler Platz. Part of the Amano hotel group, this is a smaller establishment, but just as cool. The darkly coloured interiors harmonize with the overriding influence of leather and metal. Rooms are small, but meticulously planned. Their location towards the back of the hotel keeps them well away from the busy Torstrasse. In addition to its central location, the Mani hotel offers iPods and a complementary Berlin guide, which guests receive at the hotel reception, plus the popular hotel bar and excellent breakfast buffet.

Address: Torstraße 136, 10119 Berlin
Phone: 0049 (0)30 53028080, Website: www.amanogroup.de/hotels/mani
Price: Double from €80

Hotel   Restaurant   Café   Bar   Shop   //   Interview   Interesting facts   Recipe

☞ Linnen Berlin

The Linnen Apartments are billed as a 'home away from home' – and they certainly live up to this idea. Instead of exaggerated interior design, Linnen's mantra is brightly coloured interiors, generous space and playful touches. The six rooms and four apartments are not all contained within the same building, but are distributed across various locations in Prenzlauer Berg and Mitte. The building at Prenzlauer Berg also has a wonderful café where guests can enjoy fresh juices and organic coffee.

Address: Eberswalder Straße 35, Prenzlauer Berg/
Rosa-Luxemburg-Straße 3/Große Hamburger Straße 17, Mitte
Phone: 0049 (0)30 47 372440, Website: www.linnenberlin.com
Price: Rooms/apartments from €75, minimum 2 nights

Hotel Restaurant Café Bar Shop // Interview Interesting facts Recipe

☞ Gorki Apartments

The Gorki Apartments are now probably the most luxurious and appealing venues the capital has to offer. 34 apartments and two luxurious penthouses are accommodated in an old apartment building in Mitte. The mix of classic designer furniture from names like Dixon, Eiermann and Knoll is complemented by vintage finds from local flea markets as well as modern pieces. While the apartments measure 21 to 51 square metres, the penthouses offer 185 and 200 square metres. You can live as independently as you do back home, or rely on a concierge service for a little more luxury while travelling.

Gorki Apartments Address: Weinbergsweg 25, 10119 Berlin
Phone: 0049 (0)30 48496480, Website: www.gorkiapartments.de
Price: from €115

Hotel Restaurant Café Bar Shop // Interview Interesting facts Recipe

LOKAL

Simple white walls, solid wooden tables, concrete floors, sheepskins and tall windows – the light-flooded mezzanine level at Linienstrasse is the new darling of Berlin's agency workers and those involved in the creative industry. This is a popular lunch venue serving oven-baked vegetables with quark dip or homemade pasta and carrot pesto. In the evenings when bright daylight fades to cosy lighting, Chef Gary Hoopengardner treats diners to fine German cuisine. Menu choices include fillet steak with cherry chutney, cheese and onion tartlets with beetroot, amaranth, tomatoes, strawberries or king oyster mushrooms with nettle, blackcurrant, beetroot and Brie.

Lokal evolved from the Chipperfield canteen that was originally a restaurant for David Chipperfield's architect's studio. Its fabulous cuisine and interiors helped it morph into a bustling dinner venue. The restaurant closed in 2011 and took two years to re-open – now only at lunchtimes. That was a good enough reason for Maren Thimm and her husband, Gary Hoopengardner, to open their own restaurant – an equally stylish and appealing alternative for the old canteen's regular clientele.

Lokal Address: Linienstraße 160, Mitte Phone: 0049 (0)30 28449500
Website: www.lokal-berlin.blogspot.com Opening hours:
Saturday – Monday from 5 p.m., Tuesday – Friday from 11 a.m.

Hotel Restaurant Café Bar Shop // Interview Interesting facts Recipe

An interview with Maren Thimm
Lokal restaurant owner

Your background isn't actually in the restaurant trade. How did you end up managing two restaurants?
I studied business administration, but I was always passionate about food. I'm from a family of 'foodies'. At home I'm also curious to know where my food comes from and how it's prepared. That's my passion. Then, I started with the Chipperfield canteen and, thanks to its resounding success, Gary and I opened our Lokal.

What's the idea behind Lokal?
We mainly work with local, small suppliers. We have our own herb garden and work creatively with exotic vegetable or cereal varieties. Our menu changes daily. Every day at midday we review our fresh vegetables, meat and fish and decide on the dinner menu. We also ferment, marinate and smoke many products and complement or refine our dishes using these ingredients.

What's your classic dish?
Homemade pasta with vegetables.

Where do the wonderful, naturally stained wooden tables come from?
Designer Katja Buchholz creates them. The wood is from sustainable timber sourced from the region around Berlin and the tabletop of the large 'Stammtisch' (exclusively for our regular clientele) comes from Katja's grandparent's house.

Einkorn wheat risotto

Soak the einkorn wheat the day before in salted water. Bring the einkorn to the boil in vegetable stock or water for 45 minutes. When the einkorn has the right consistency, add the Riesling and goat's cheese crème fraîche.

Bring the redcurrant juice and a pinch of salt to the boil until it reduces by half. Add the xanthan and combine everything using a hand blender. Stir in the goat's milk yoghurt shortly before serving.

Wash the vegetables. Break the cauliflower into bite-size pieces. Cut the Romano peppers lengthways in the middle and remove the seeds. Grate the fennel with a cheese grater and mix with a little apple vinegar and salt.

Heat a pan with butter and lightly fry the cauliflower and pepper. Then put the vegetables in a hot oven. Heat a frying pan with a dash of oil and sauté the spinach with a little nutmeg and pepper. Serve the einkorn wheat risotto with the vegetables and the redcurrant reduction. Garnish with fresh dill, wild herbs and crumble blue cheese over the top.

Einkorn wheat:
500 g einkorn wheat
100 g goat's cheese crème fraîche
150 ml Riesling
salt

Redcurrant reduction:
1 l redcurrant juice
1 g xanthan gum
1 tbsp goat's milk yoghurt

Vegetables:
1 cauliflower
2 Romano peppers
1 fennel root
apple vinegar & salt
250 g fresh spinach
nutmeg & pepper
Blue cheese
Dill & wild herbs

Hotel Restaurant Café Bar Shop // Interview Interesting facts Recipe

☞ Chipperfield Canteen

Berlin breathed a sigh of relief when the brand-new Chipperfield canteen reopened; its predecessor had become a firm favourite with the locals in Mitte. The new concept from the Lokal team has scored another hit. Every day the reasonably priced menu has three different main courses and starters. The clean and tastefully finished concrete interiors reflect meticulous attention to design details. It's worth setting off for lunch early – latecomers will be disappointed to find that the restaurant is already full.

Address: Joachimstraße 11, 10119 Berlin, Phone: 0049 (0)30 33844430
Opening hours: Monday–Friday 8:30 a.m. – 8 p.m.
(Lunch: noon – 3 p.m.)

Hotel Restaurant Café Bar Shop // Interview Interesting facts Recipe

Sale e Tabacchi

Sale e Tabacchi is a classic Berlin restaurant renowned for its long-standing exceptional quality. It's worth a visit just to experience the rooms inside. Bathed in natural daylight and with clean architectural lines, the interiors never seem outdated.

This is the perfect venue to meet for a midday business lunch. An extensive menu offers great value with contemporary, authentic Italian dishes. The starters are particularly delicious. Try the Parmigiana, or 'pure di fave secche con cicoria' – a bean purée with chicory, Parmesan and chilli, which is unique to Berlin. Or sample fresh artichokes with mint and garlic, and homemade ravioli with a spinach and ricotta filling – almost better tasting than in Italy!

In the evening the atmosphere is glamorous without being too posh. Well-educated, politically minded people from all over the city frequent this place. Another telltale sign of professional restaurateurship is when you recognize the familiar faces of waiting staff who have worked here for years.

Sale e Tabacchi Address: Rudi-Dutschke-Straße 18, Kreuzberg
Phone: 0049 (0)30 2521155 Website: www.sale-e-tabacchi.de
Opening hours: Daily from 10 a.m. till late

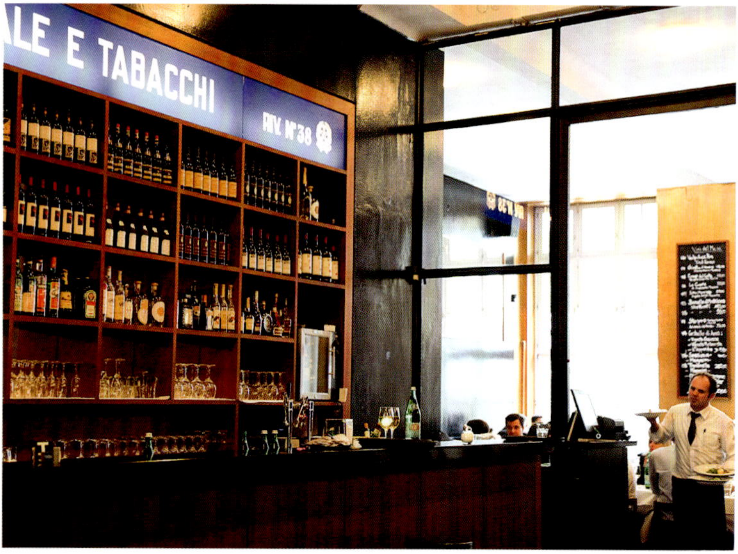
ALE E TABACCHI
RIV. N°38

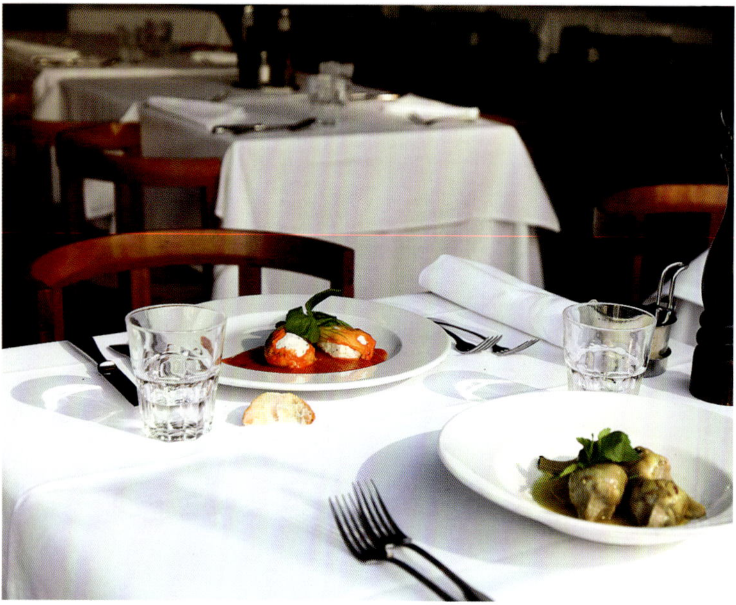

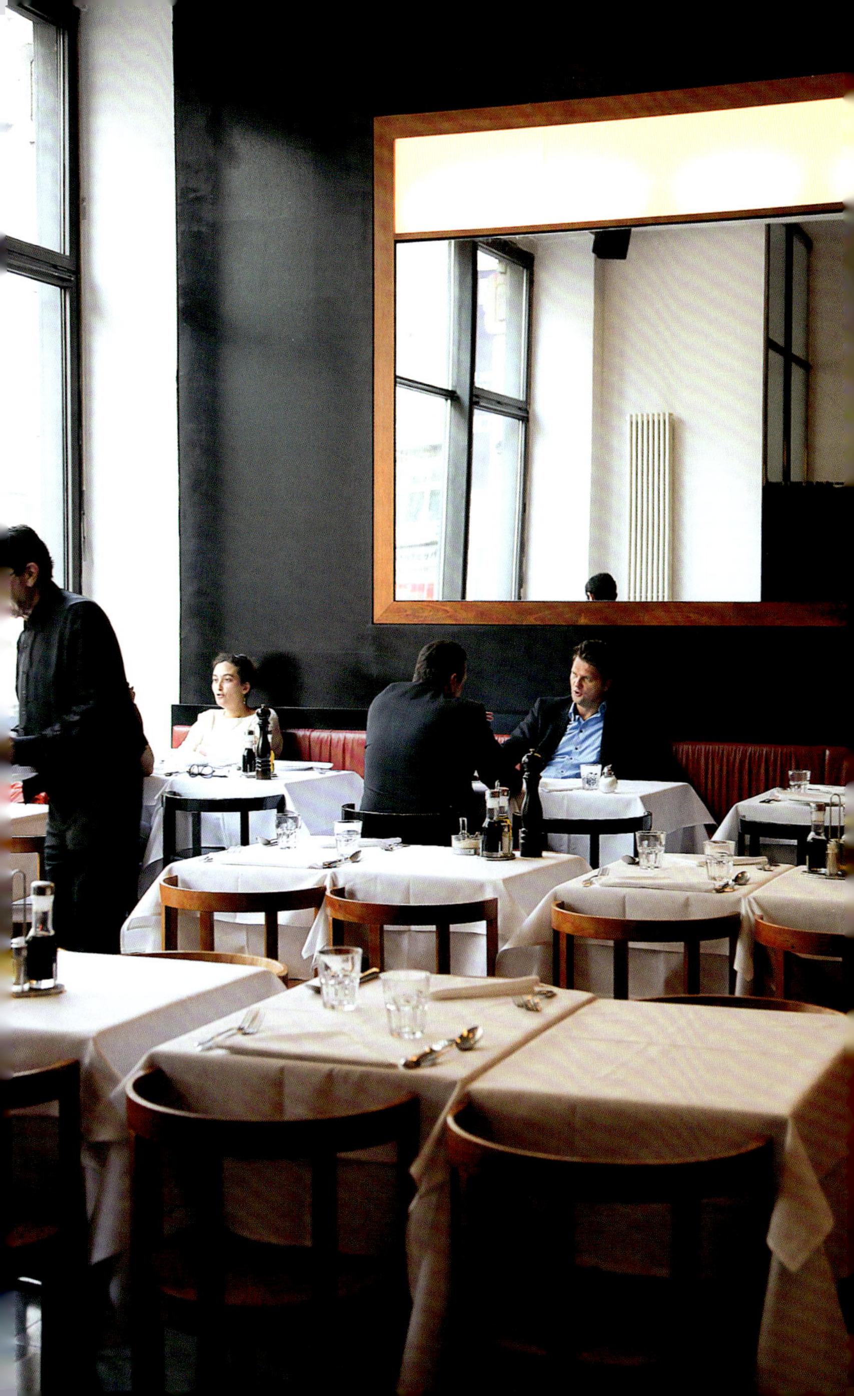

☞ Westberlin Cafe

Westberlin offers coffee, cake and magazines – that's according to the advertising board on the pavement, and it's certainly true. The café towards the quieter end of Friedrichstrasse, bordering on Kreuzberg, is part café and part media shop. Yet, the emphasis is on coffee – Fair Trade and organic, of course. The baristas really know how to make a great coffee and they take every care with the preparation. The interiors are bright, friendly and reminiscent of cafés in Copenhagen or Stockholm.

Address: Friedrichstraße 215, 10969 Berlin
Phone: 0049 (0)30 25922745, Website: www.westberlin-bar-shop.de
Opening hours: Monday – Friday 8:30 a.m. – 7 p.m.,
Saturday 10 a.m. – 7 p.m., Sunday noon – 5 p.m.

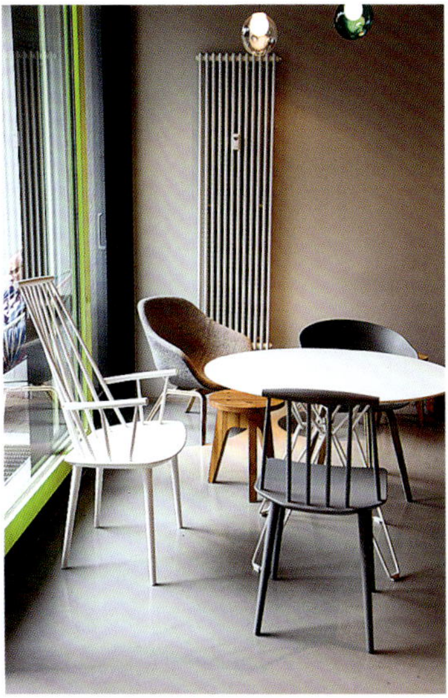

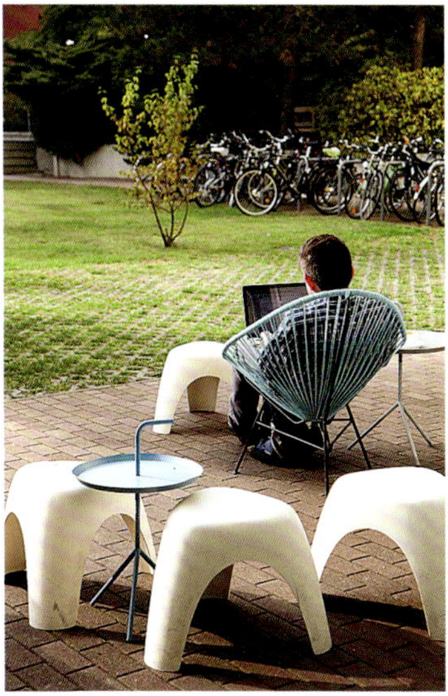

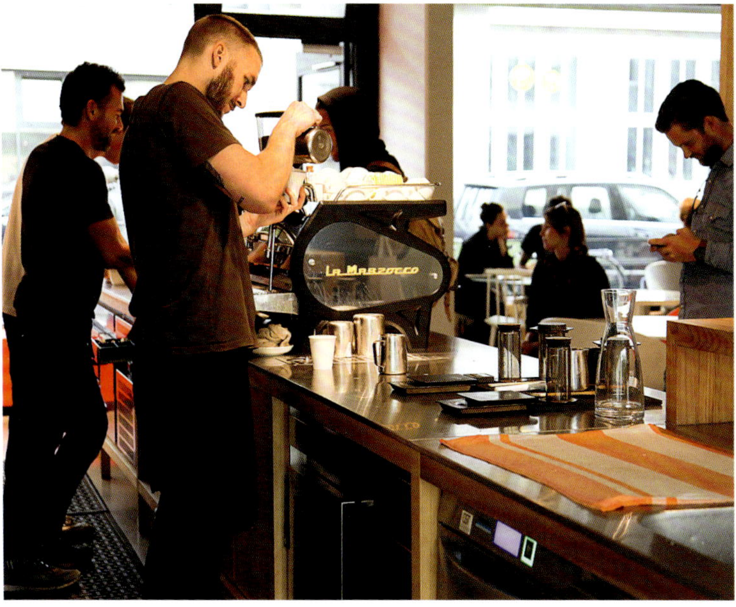
La Marzocco

Hotel Restaurant Café Bar Shop // Interview Interesting facts Recipe

☞ Borchardt

If you consider the Gendarmenmarkt Berlin's dining salon, then you could say that the Borchardt supplies the cuisine. This is Karl Lagerfeld's favourite restaurant whenever he is in Berlin; it's a regular choice for government officials, a rendez-vous for the media, stars of the catwalk, Adel as well as popular with ordinary Berliners and travellers. Everybody feels the exciting lure of the clientele. Borchardt stands for cosmopolitan-style bistro food. Regulars enjoy their favourite dishes every day. Popular classics like oysters, rib-eye steak with béarnaise sauce, Wiener schnitzel, black pudding and crème brûlée of foie gras are permanently on the menu. Side orders like crispy vegetables, gratin or a miscellany of salads can be added as extras. Seasonal asparagus or chanterelles also appear on the menu. You can always count on variety, too, so any special dietary requirements are catered for. The Borchardt isn't only about high-quality food – although after some past ups and downs, nowadays it's hard to fault the quality. Seeing and being seen take priority as do chatting with confidantes in a private alcove, or sitting outdoors on the terrace with friends in summer and feeling the city's beat. It's all about participating in Berlin's exhilarating vibe!

Address: Französische Straße 47, Mitte
Phone: 0049 (0)30 81886262, Website: www.borchardt-restaurant.de
Opening hours: Daily 11:30 a.m. – midnight
Tip: Reservations are essential at peak dining time.

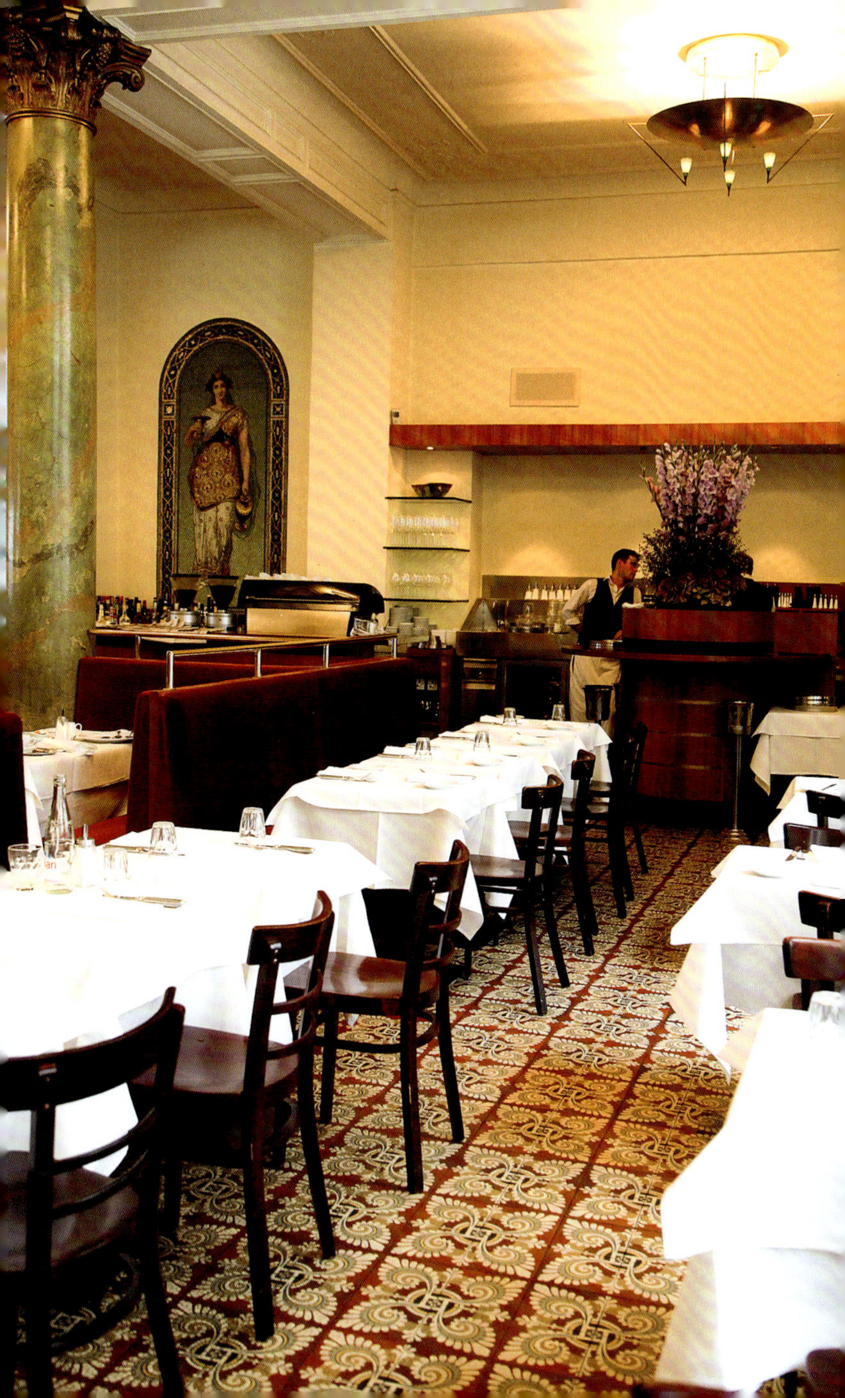

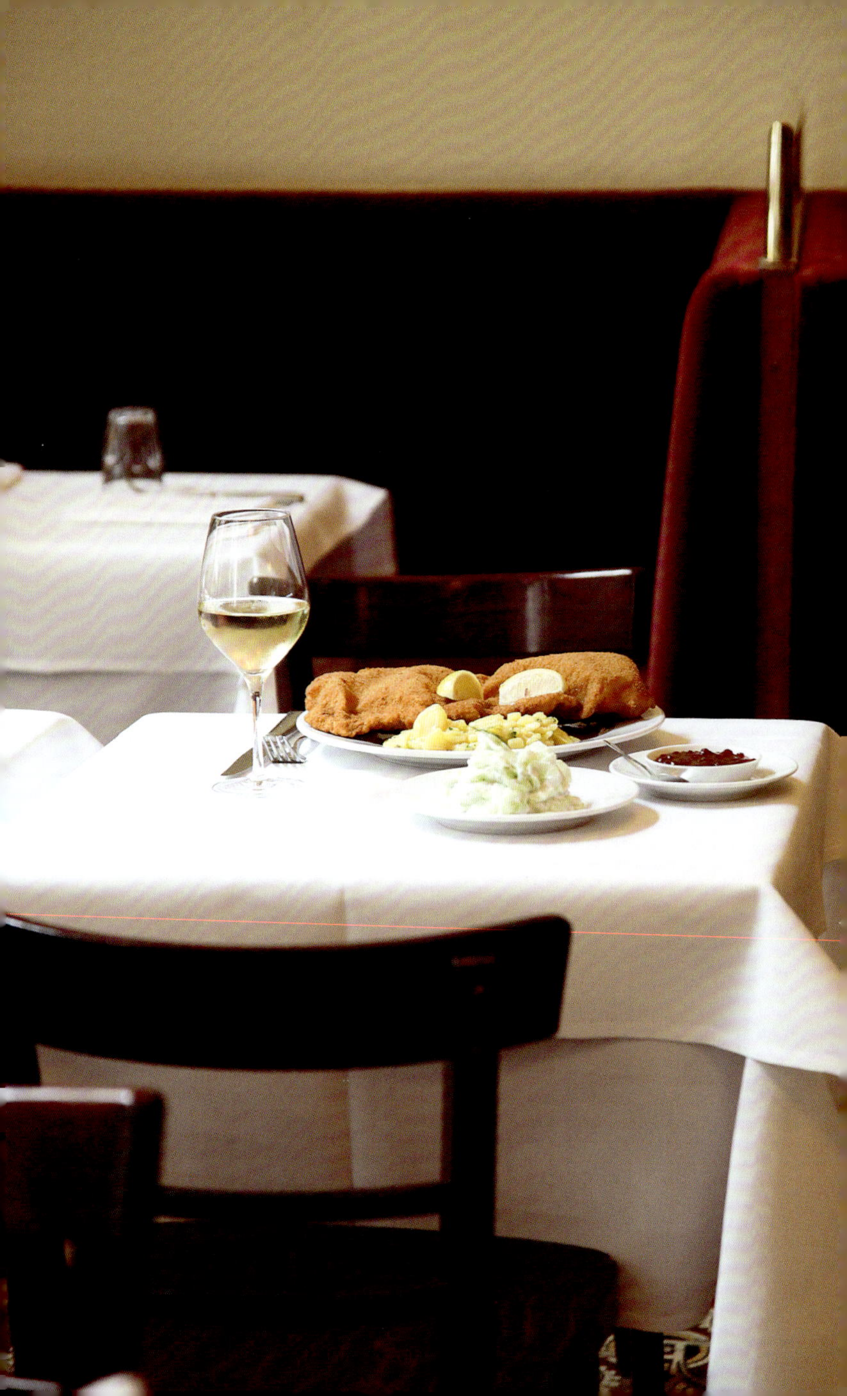

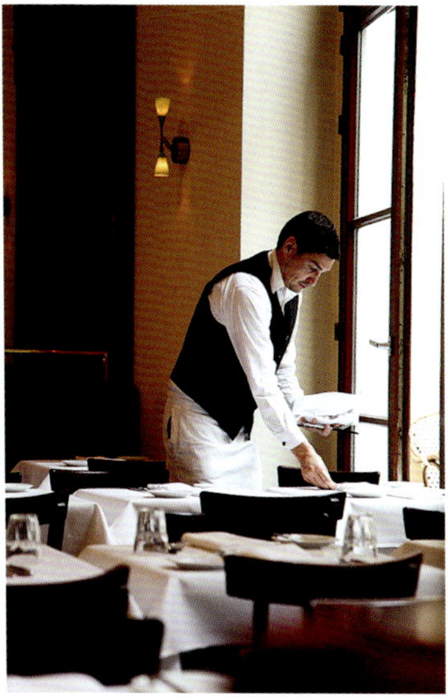
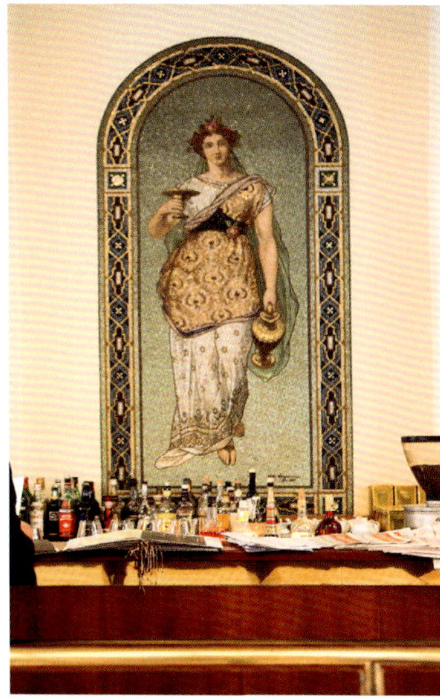
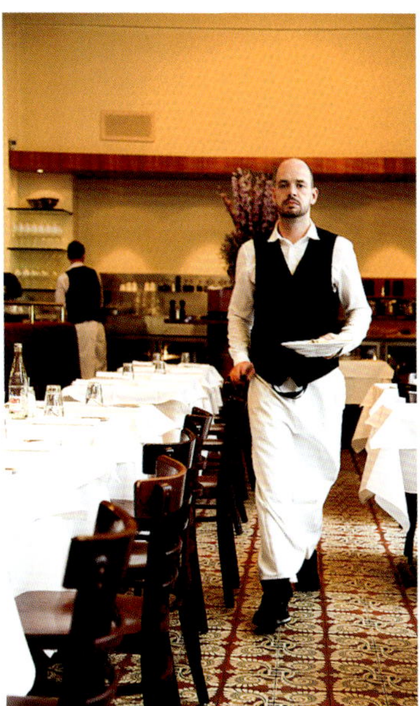
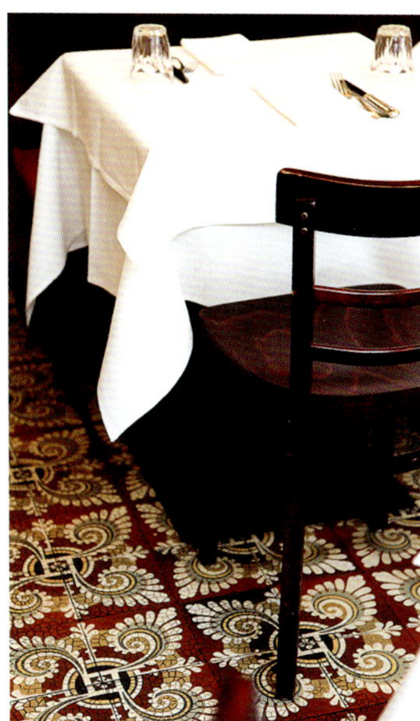

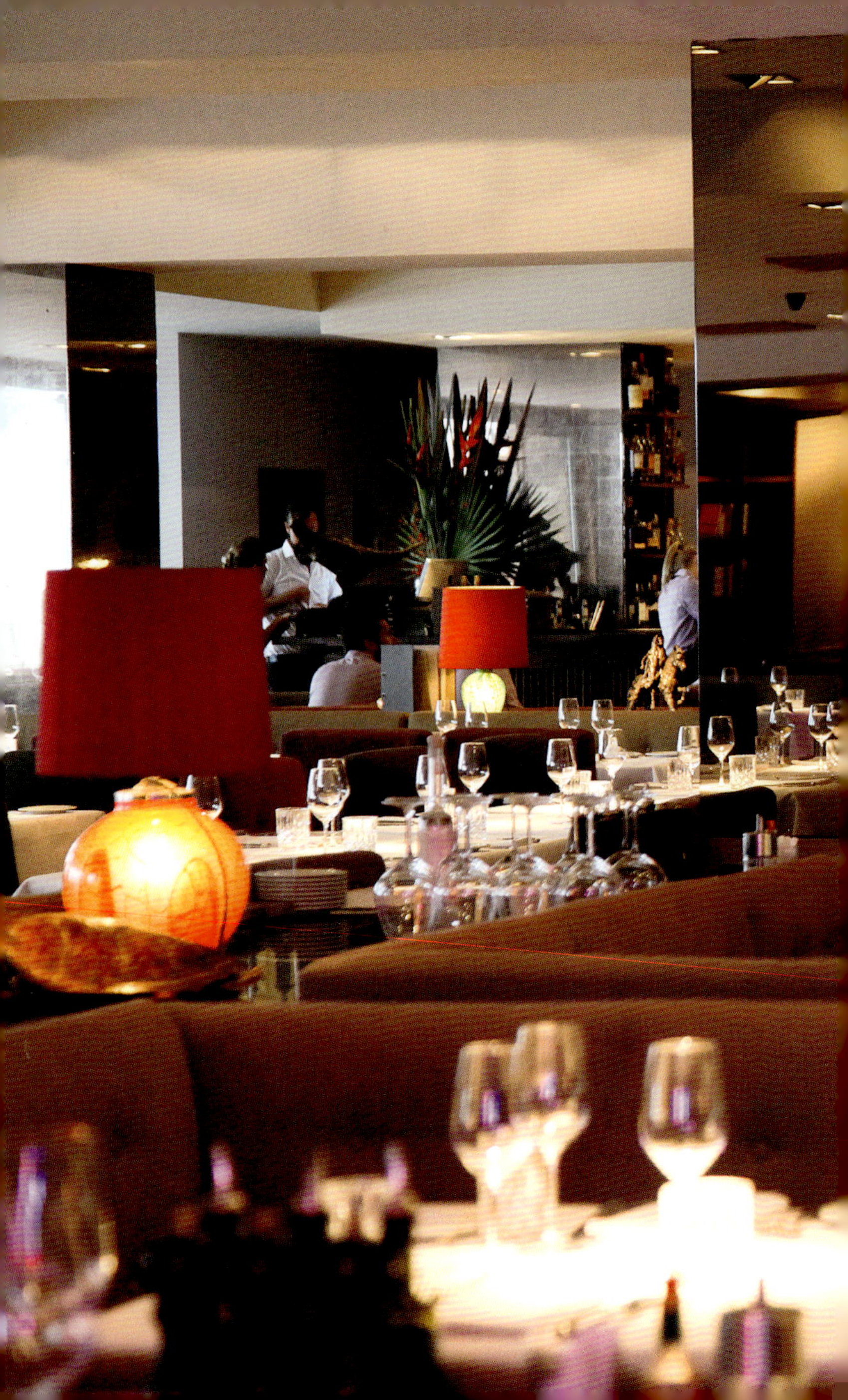

GRILL ROYAL

GRILL ROYAL

Borchardt, Paris Bar or more recently Grill Royal – opinion is divided on which restaurant is the best and in highest demand. One thing is certain – this trendy establishment run by Boris Radczun and Stefan Landwehr definitely ranks top of the list of Berlin restaurants. Finding anywhere better than the spacious terrace overlooking the Spree is already tricky enough. Indoors, the spacious rooms are just as impressive and reminiscent of a 1960s American film set. Plush and luxurious alcoves, white tablecloths, red table lamps for demure lighting combine with the gentle flow of the River Spree outside. Here, you can sit back and anticipate what's next – and it is delicious. Meatlovers, in particular will get their money's worth here. The beef sourced from three world regions is exceptional and the fish is equally exquisite. Everything is served to perfection. Sauces and side orders can be added individually. An absolute must: the crispy French fries and sweet-potato crisps. The Grill – as Berliners call it – is the ideal venue to enjoy an evening with a large group of friends. Here, Berlin's beautiful people rub shoulders with arty individuals and international celebrities meet tourists.

Grill Royal   Address: Friedrichstraße 105 b, Mitte
Phone: 0049 (0)30 28879288   Website: www.grillroyal.com
Opening hours: Daily from 6 pm

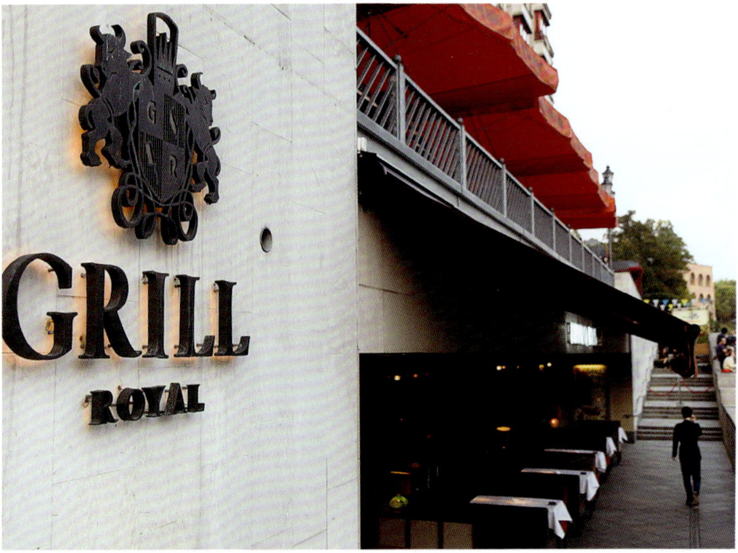
GRILL
ROYAL

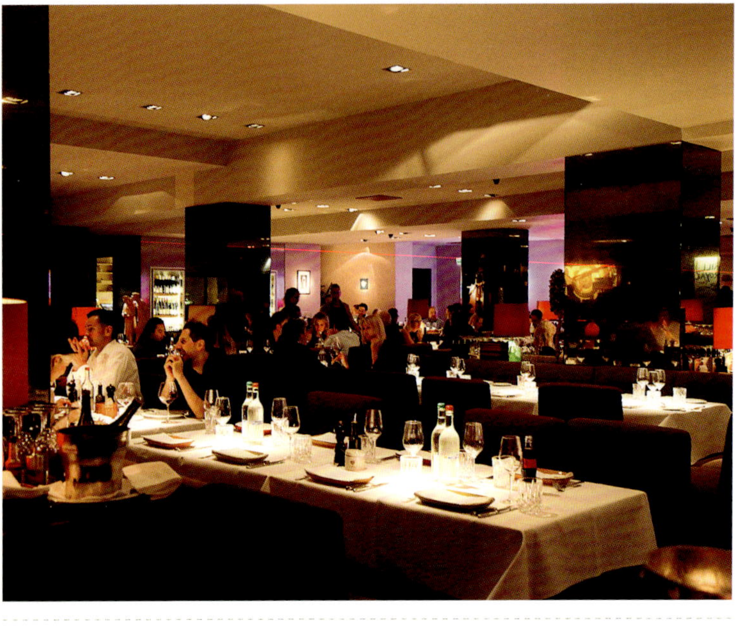

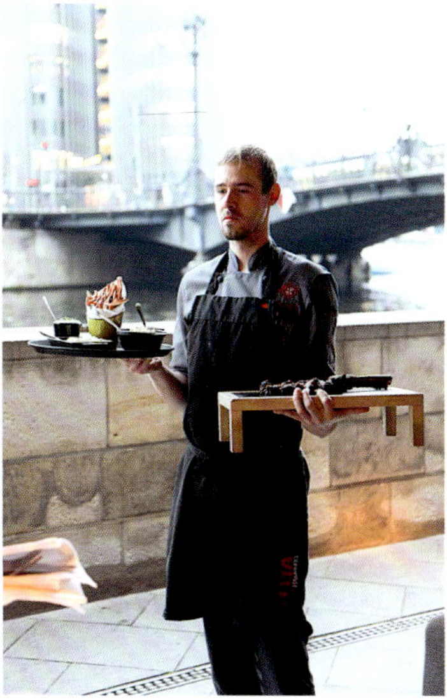

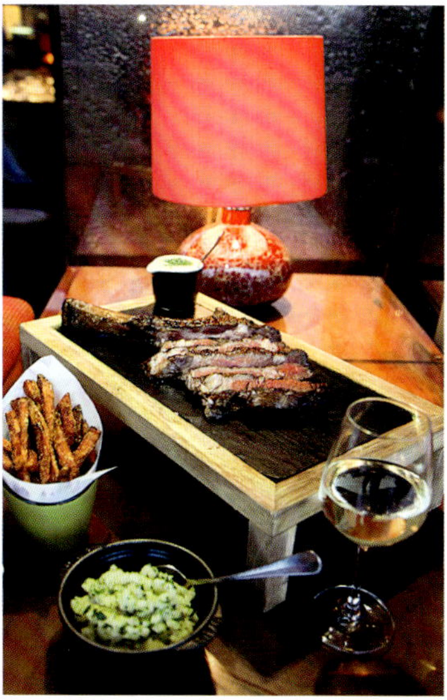

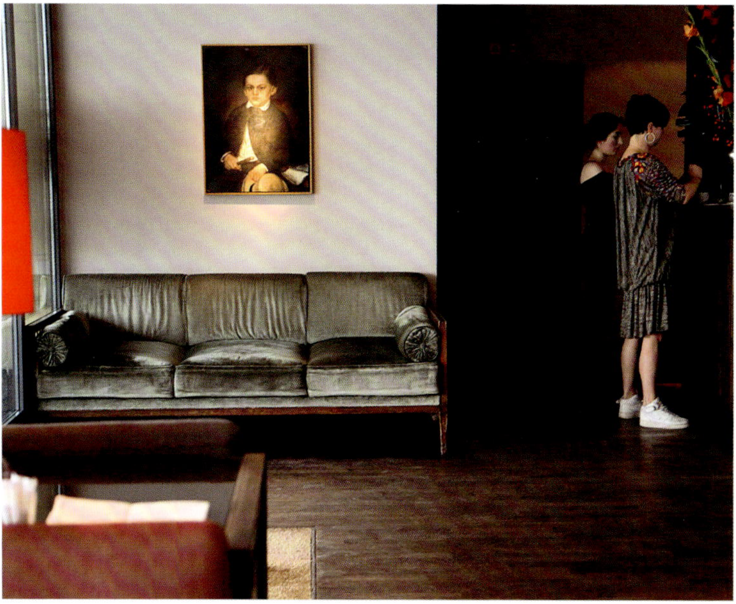

Hotel Restaurant Café Bar Shop // Interview Interesting facts Recipe

☞ Pauly Saal

Pauly Saal, one of Berlin Mitte's most stylish meeting places, attracts business people, art lovers and the 'who's who' of Berlin's in-crowd as well as the city's international visitors. The trend-setting restaurant is located in the premises of a former Jewish girls' school in a wonderful brick building that now also houses several art galleries. Before venturing into the opulent dining hall, you should set foot in the restaurant bar where you can sip a gin and tonic and soak up the relaxed lounge atmosphere. Then, take a seat on moss green cushions at tables decked out with white linen and enjoy some exceptional German cuisine beneath Pauly Saal's trademark – a giant red rocket.

Address: Auguststraße 11-13, Mitte, Phone: 0049 (0)30 33006070
Website: www.paulysaal.com, Opening hours: Daily from noon till late

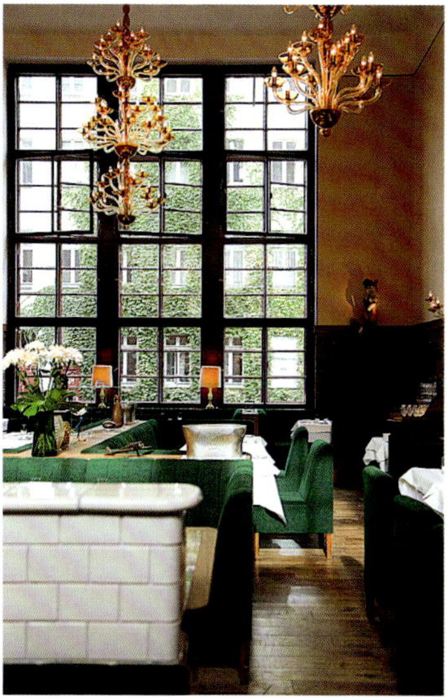

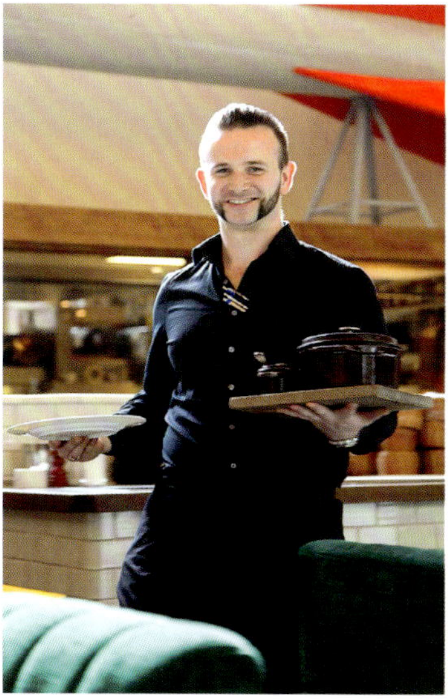

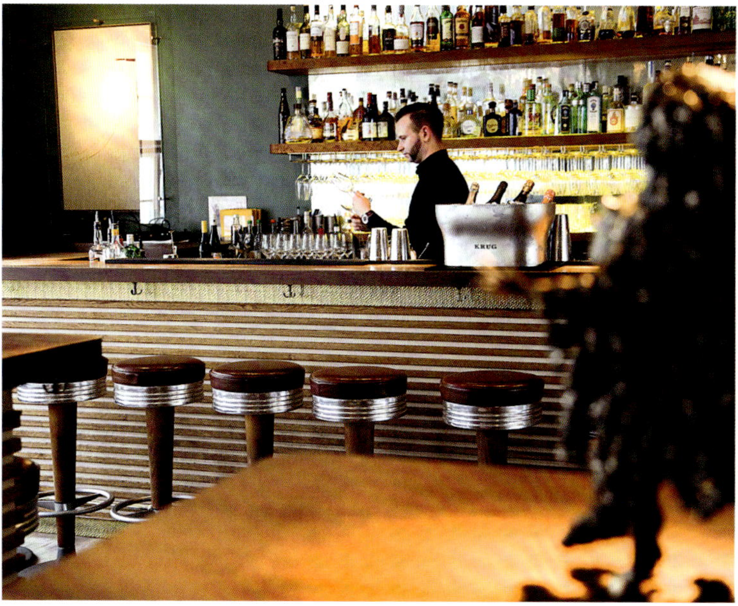
KRUG

Hotel Restaurant Café Bar Shop // Interview Interesting facts Recipe

☞ Mogg & Melzer

At last, the hot-selling Pastrami sandwiches, which we know and love from Katz in New York, have also made it to Berlin. That's a real stroke of luck! Owners Paul Mogg & Oskar Melzer spent years testing the range of Pastrami hams; they tried everything until their Pastrami was as mouthwatering as it is today. The cheesecake is one of their grandmother's old recipes, and the very few dishes on the menu are naturally Jewish and kosher. You cannot access the deli from the street – go through the main entrance of Pauly Saal.

Address: Auguststraße 11-13, Mitte, Phone: 0049 (0)30 330060770
Website: www.moggandmelzer.com, Monday – Friday 8 a.m. till late,
Saturday and Sunday 10 a.m. till late

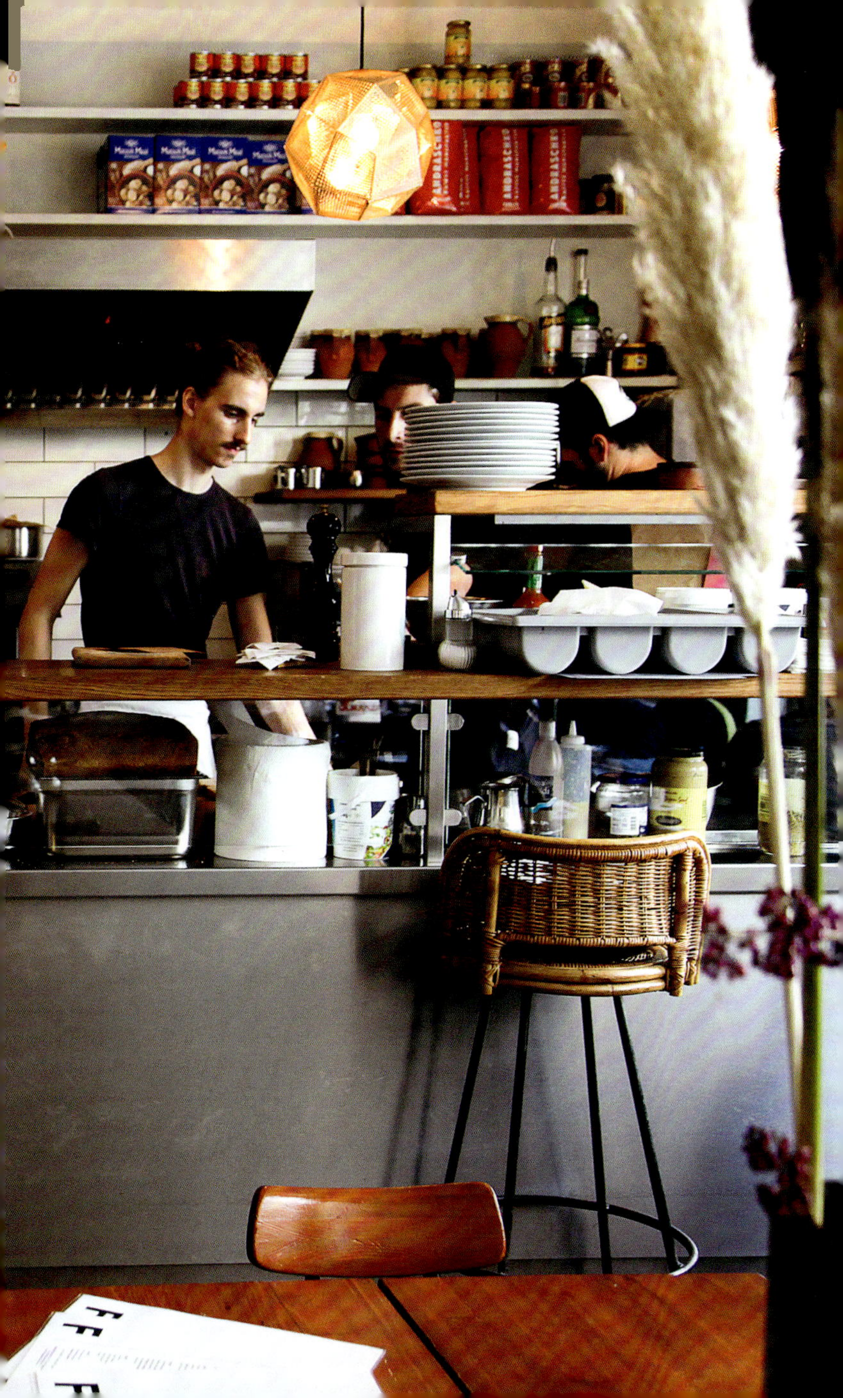

COOKIES
CREAM

Hotel Restaurant Café Bar Shop // Interview Interesting facts Recipe

COOKIES CREAM

COOKIES CREAM

Cookies Cream restaurant belongs to Berlin's legendary Cookies nightclub. In 2014, after 20 years, the nightclub closed, but the restaurant keeps alive a spirit of exuberance and a slightly down-at-heel atmosphere that also epitomizes Berlin. Finding your way here is actually quite an adventure – via the rear courtyard of Berlin's Komische Oper and up a shabby staircase, leading to the first floor. But once you have crossed the threshold, the ambiance changes instantly. You find yourself inside an elegant factory with rough exposed concrete ceilings, whitewashed brick walls, retro furniture and stylishly laid tables. Cookies Cream is one of Berlin's trendiest venues. An important point to note is the 100% vegetarian menu with a wide selection of vegan food. Dishes are seasonal and prepared with regional products. The innovate use of vegetable and herb varieties has also arrived here. Typical sample menus are goat's cheese mousse with braised cucumber, garnished with cherry halves and seasoned with lovage, or smoked Jerusalem artichoke with watercress and mustard.

The Cream Bar is a recent addition and serves classic drinks with a modern twist. Rumour has it that the former nightclub could make a comeback soon – read more about this in the next book.

Cookies Cream Address: Behrenstraße 55, Mitte
Phone: 0049 (0)30 27492940 Website: www.cookies-cream.com
Opening hours: In summer, Tuesday to Saturday: from 7 p.m.,
in winter from 6 p.m.

ficken

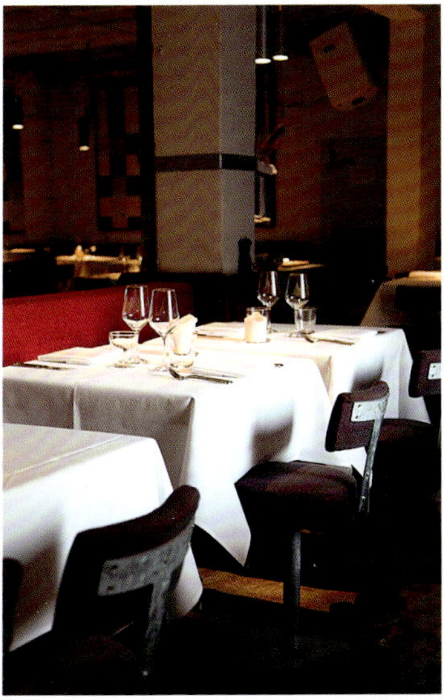
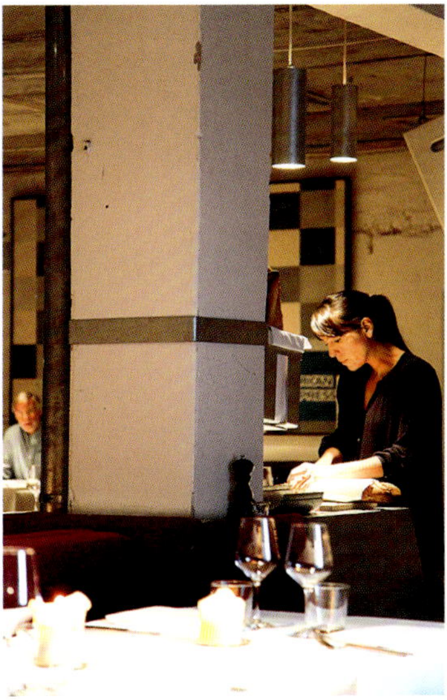
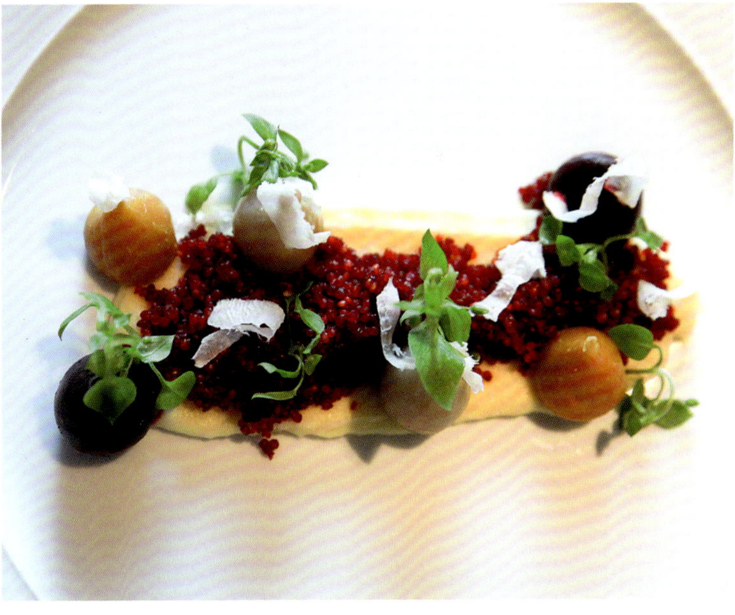

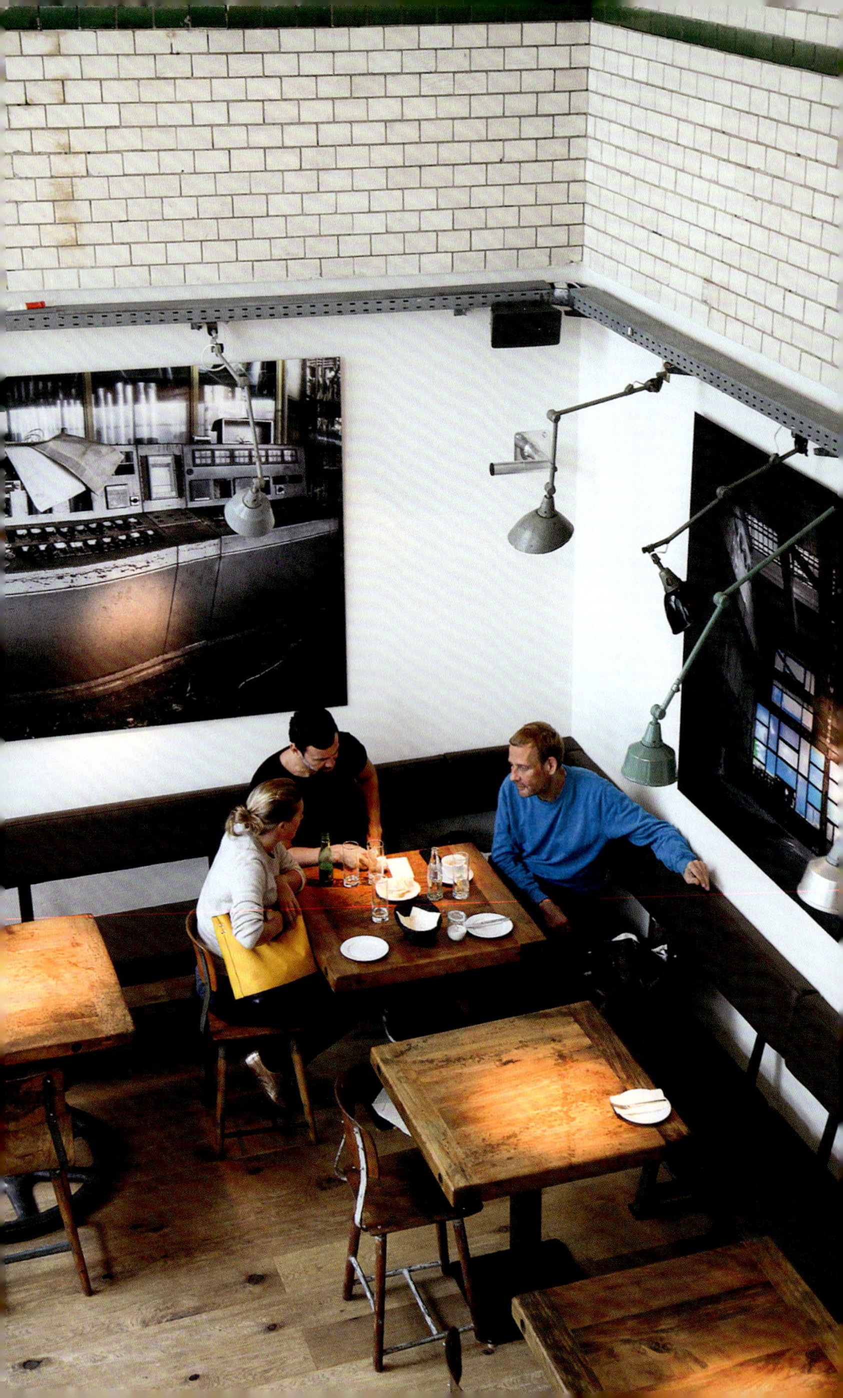

Hotel Restaurant Café Bar Shop // Interview Interesting facts Recipe

EINS44 KANTINE

You certainly have to know where this restaurant is to find it. Tucked away in a secluded rear courtyard of a building in Neukölln, you would never imagine a restaurant of this calibre here. The former distillery with high ceilings, huge arched windows and green and white tiles, which reach from floor to ceiling, offers a fitting backdrop for a restaurant whose industrial charm is attuned to the zeitgeist. Guest seating on wooden chairs and tables evokes memories of bygone school days. Industrial lighting gives the canteen a warm and cosy atmosphere. Three native Berliners opened the restaurant in April 2014: Sebastian Radtke (Chef de Cuisine), Jonathan Kartenberg (Restaurant Manager) and Richard Otto Reichel. After so much design perfection, your high expectations of the food are well founded. A French-inspired evening menu is based on regionally sourced ingredients and international influences. Try the black pudding with balsamic vinegar and pumpkin, or halibut with chorizo and clams or even Barbary duck with red cabbage and dumplings. The wine list is first-class with many German names from famous household labels to small vintners whose wines are worth getting to know. The lunch menu is simpler with traditional German cooking that is just as good. The Königsberger Klopse (traditional meatballs with white sauce and capers) are highly recommended.

---

eins44 Kantine Address: Elbestraße 28/29, Neukölln
Phone: 0049 (0)30 62981212 Website: www.eins44.com Opening hours: Lunch Tuesday – Friday noon – 3 p.m., evenings Tuesday – Saturday 7 p.m. – midnight Price: 3-course set menu €33, 5-course set menu €51

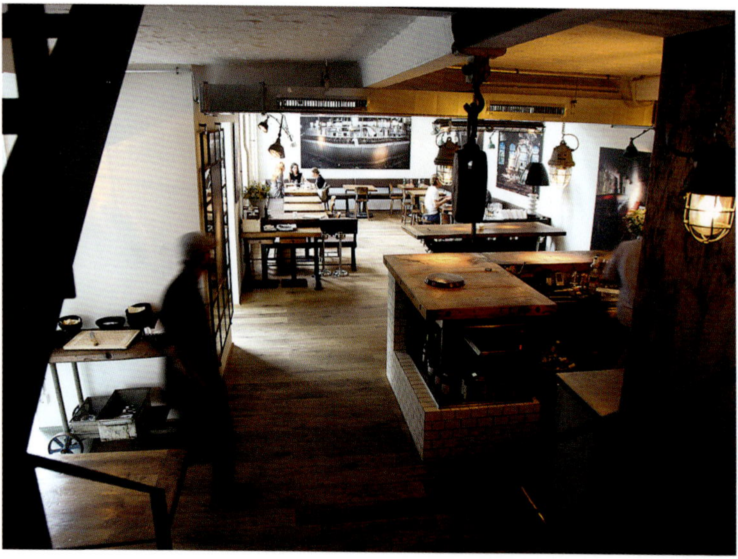

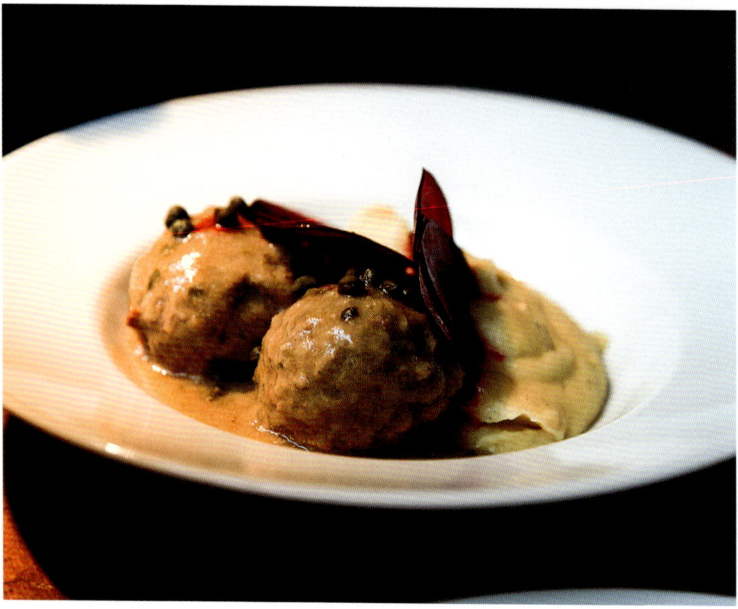

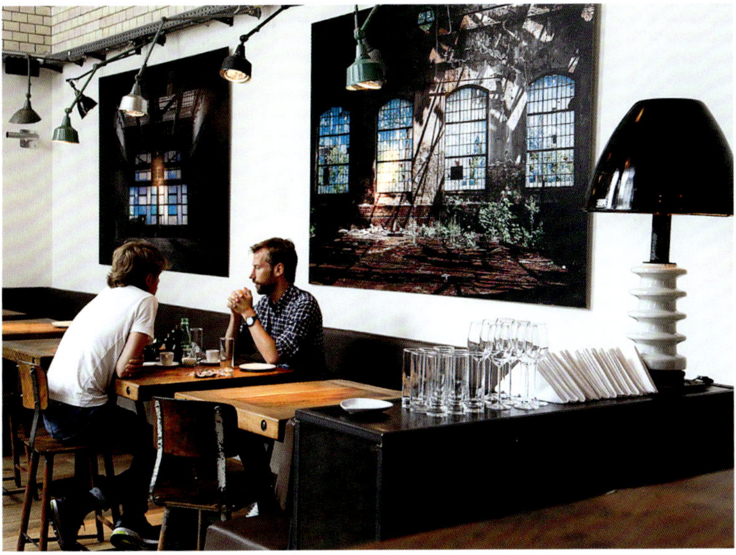

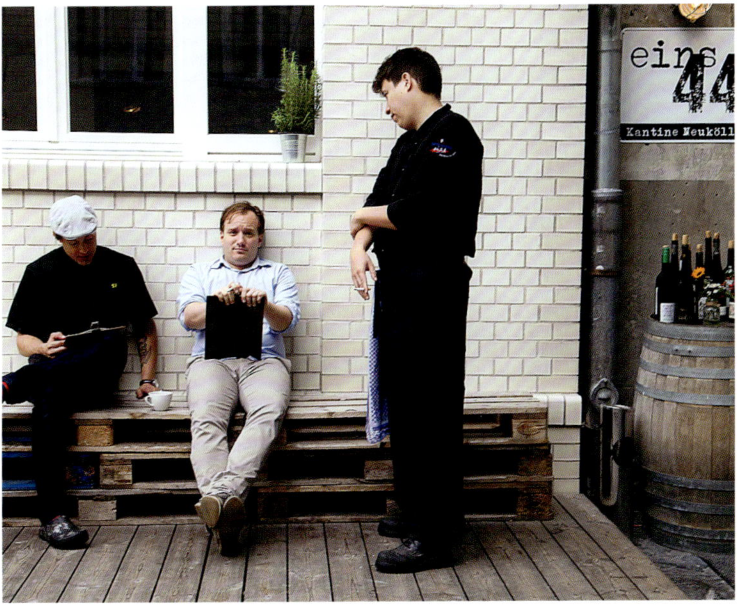
eins 44
Kantine Neukölln

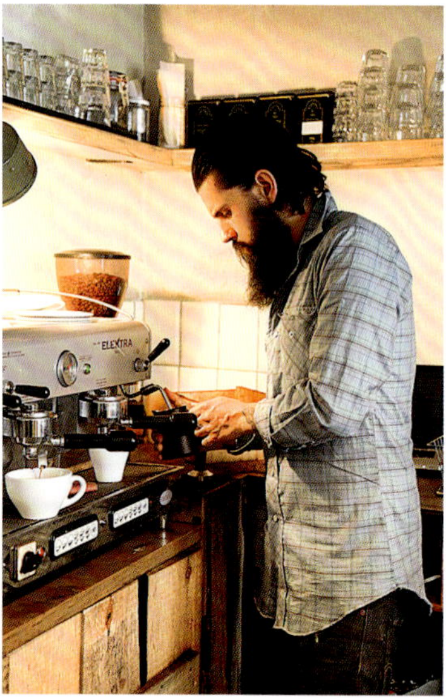

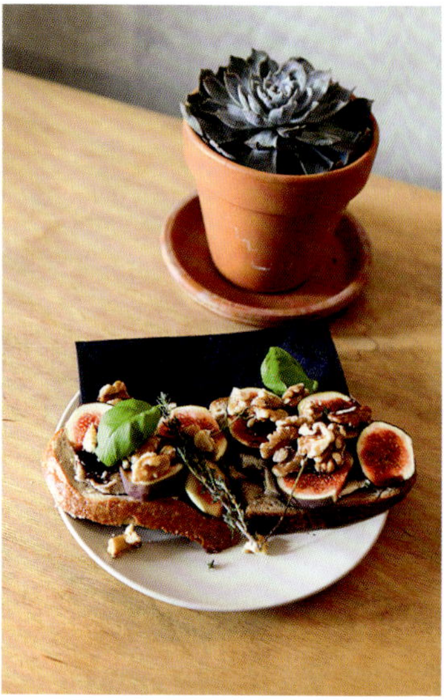

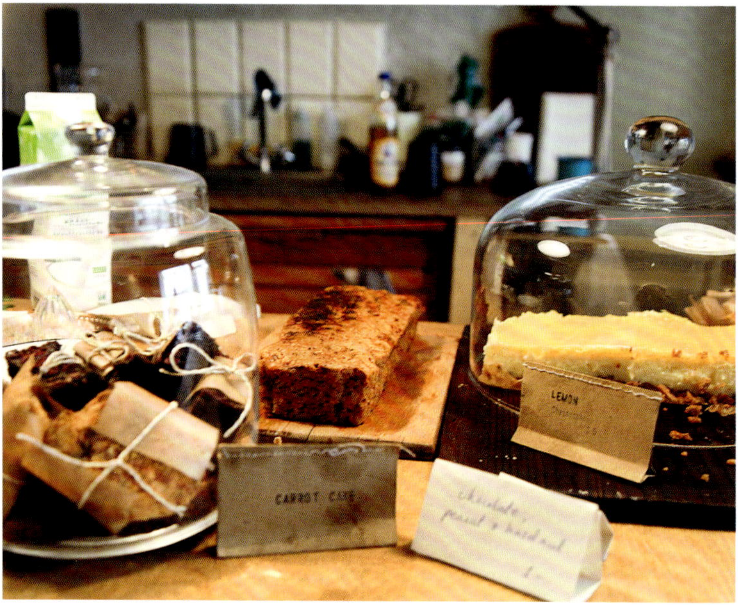
LEMON
CARROT CAKE

Hotel   Restaurant   Café   Bar   Shop   //   Interview   Interesting facts   Recipe

☞ Roamers

Roamers is an arty café in Neukölln that has a popular following with freelancers and those working in the creative world. It opens in the mornings for energy boosting, freshly squeezed juices and Bircher muesli; at midday for the grilled veggie platter or a light snack like a raspberry and banana muffin. Some customers at Roamers settle in for the day and take advantage of the free Wifi or immerse themselves in an interesting book. The homemade wooden bar, small plant pots and vintage objects on display create the cosy 'shabby chic' atmosphere.

Address: Pannierstraße 64, Neukölln
Website: www.roamersberlin.tumblr.com
Opening hours: Tuesday – Friday 9 a.m.– 7 p.m.,
Saturday and Sunday 10 a.m. – 8 p.m.

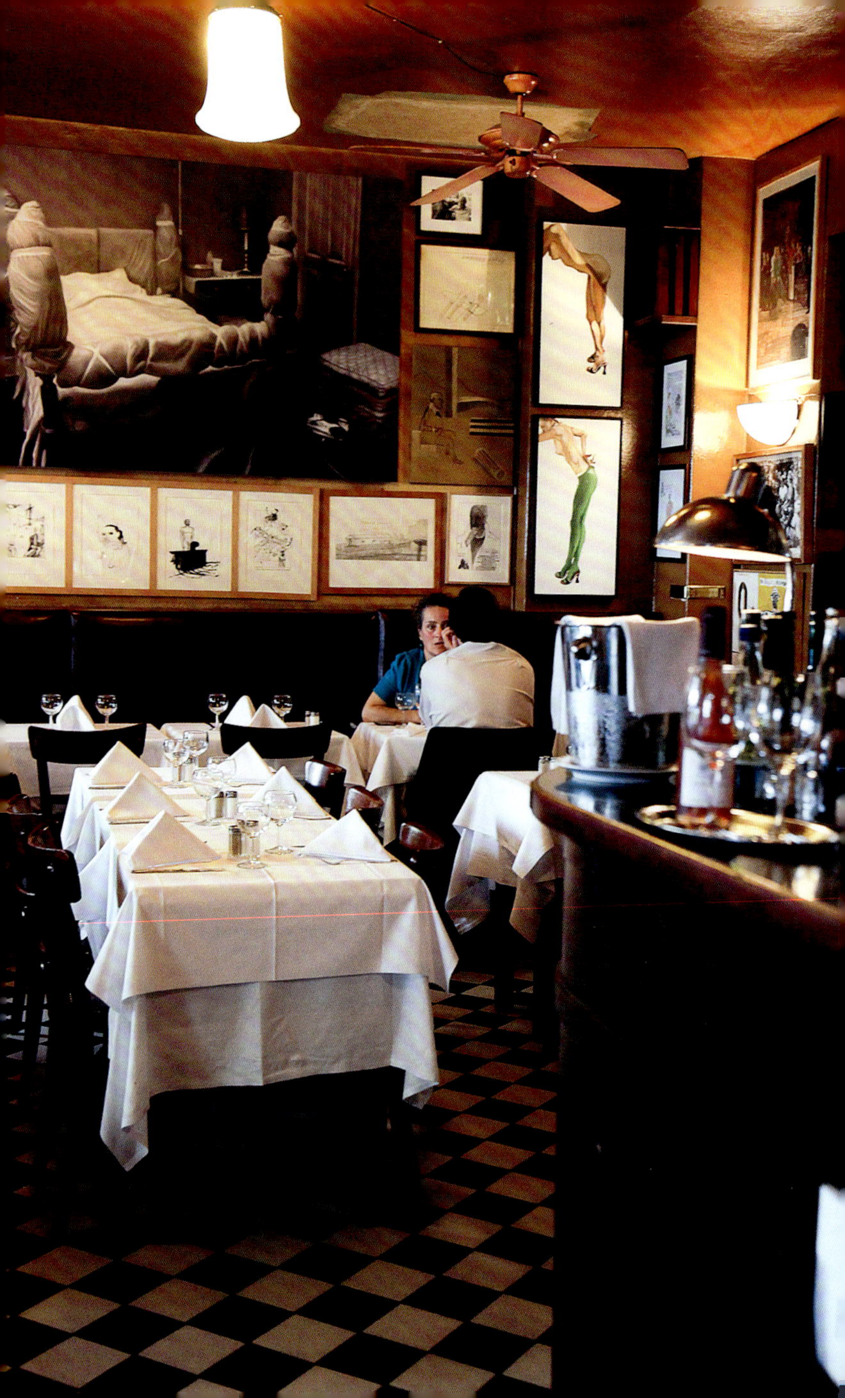

Paris Bar

PARIS BAR

Paris Bar is a Berlin institution. Regulars here swear that not even Paris can boast such an amazing and legendary café. For over 60 years this was a favourite meeting place for famous names in West Berlin, where the gallerists sipped a glass of red wine and mused about the latest trends on the art market and partied through the night with the artists. The walls are plastered with their artworks. A large Martin Kippenberger mural decorated the main wall for a long time – the work was auctioned for financial reasons and raised a respectable 2.7 million euros.

Otherwise, the French style interiors are combined with dark wooden furniture, white table linen and black and white tiled floors. Steak and French fries, steak tartare or salad Niçoise are on the menu – not even the French can do better than that. The waiters are famously arrogant which is part of the experience.

Follow the example of Berlin's artistic crowd and get here in the evening for an extended dinner with friends, or arrive in the afternoon after a shopping spree in the West to sip champagne and slurp oysters. Paris Bar is also exactly right when a mood of nostalgia takes over and a solitary glass of red wine is especially welcome.

Paris Bar   Address: Kantstraße 152, Charlottenburg
Phone: 0049 (0)30 3138052   Website: www.parisbar.net
Opening hours: Daily noon – 2:00 a.m.

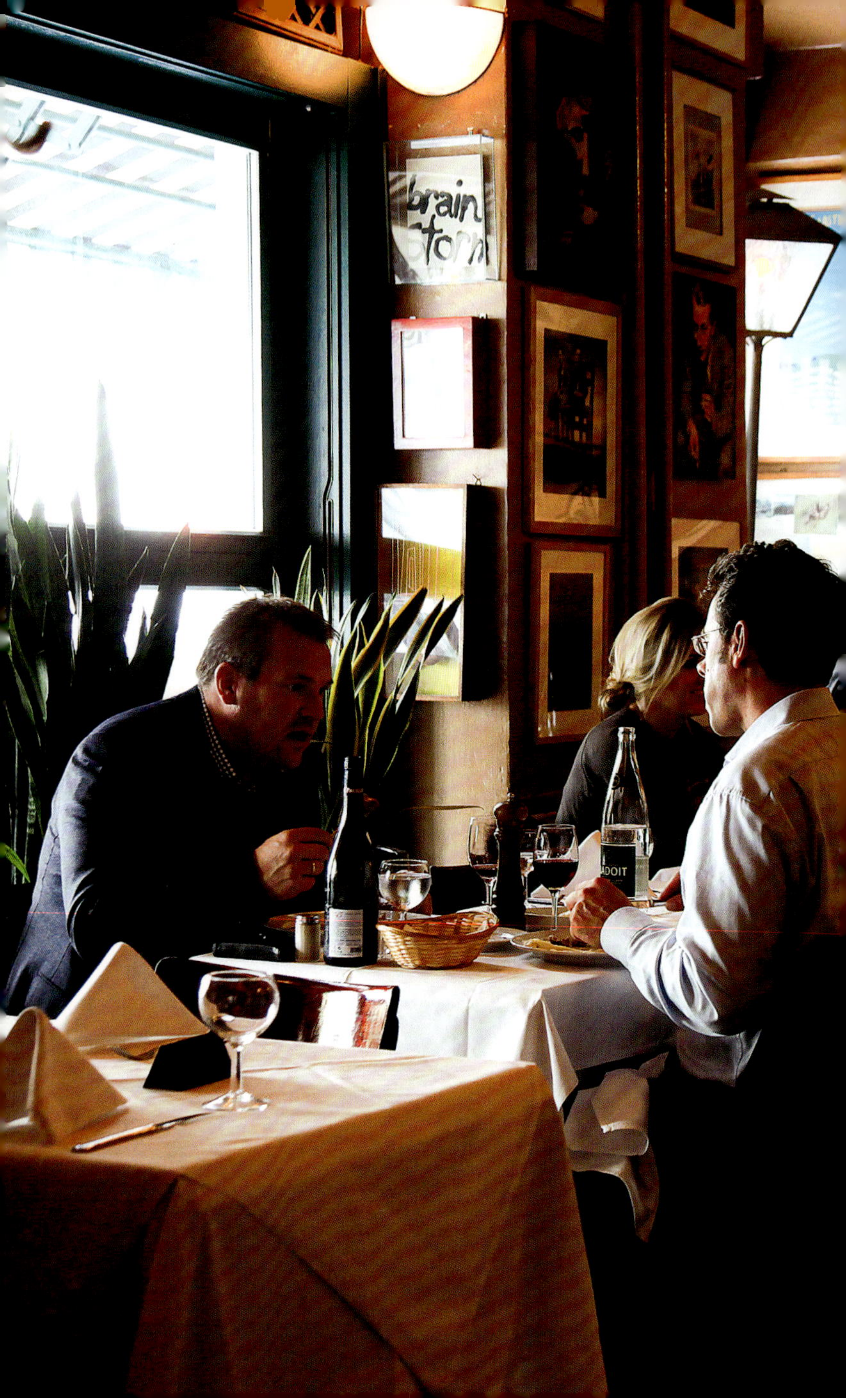
brain
ADOIT

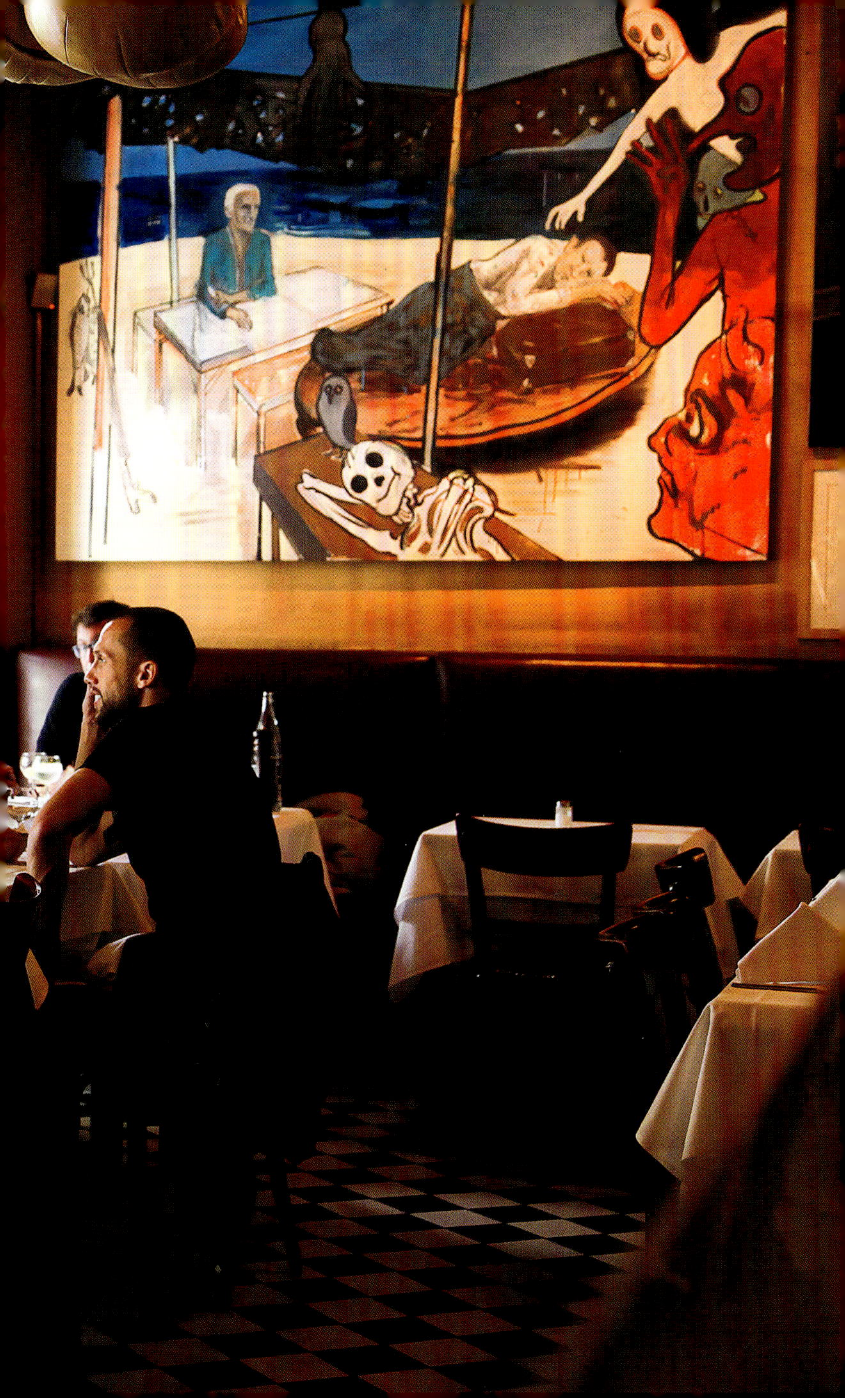

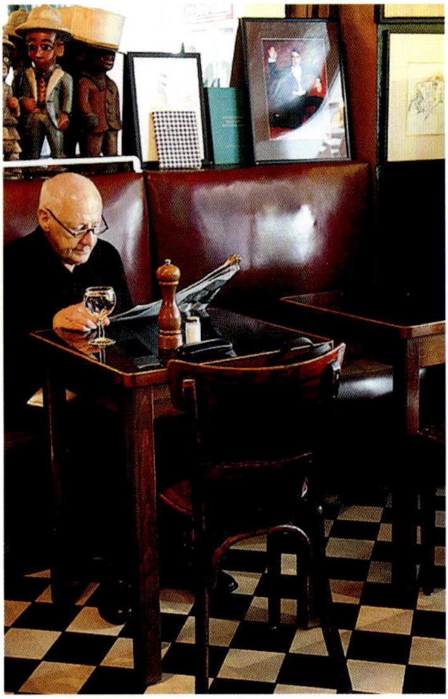

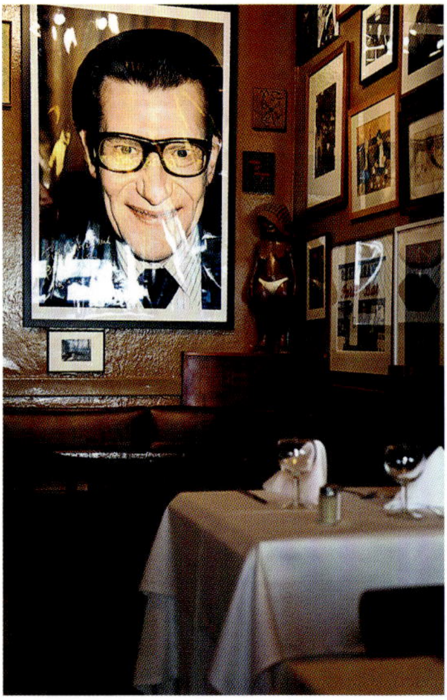

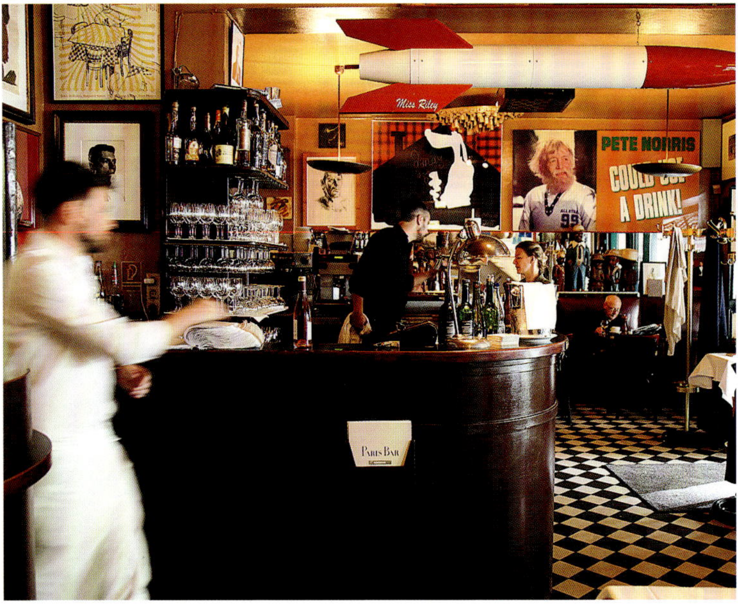
Miss Riley
PETE NORRIS
COULD
A DRINK!
Paris Bar

Hotel Restaurant Café Bar Shop // Interview Interesting facts Recipe

☞ Florian

The atmosphere in Florian is always relaxed. An older clientele of art lovers and culture vultures frequents the restaurant – and they still know how to enjoy life. Owner Florian Geyer has maintained a friendly service and an exceptionally high standard of cuisine for many years. This is the perfect venue for spending an evening with friends well into the small hours.

Grolmanstraße 52, Charlottenburg
Phone: 0049 (0)30 3139184, Website: www.restaurant-florian.de
Opening hours: Daily 6.00 p.m. – 3.00 a.m.

☞ Manzini

Manzini is the ideal choice for breakfast or lunch in the West. You can sit on the comfortable leather benches inside or outdoors in summer on the terrace where Ludwigkirchstrasse makes a pleasant backdrop. The food and beverages are high standard – eggs served in a glass or delicious club sandwiches, the ever-popular saffron and spinach risotto and classic Manzini fish soup.

Address: Ludwigkirchstraße 11, Wilmersdorf
Phone: 0049 (0)30 8857820, Website: www.manzini.de
Opening hours: Daily 8 a.m. – 2 a.m

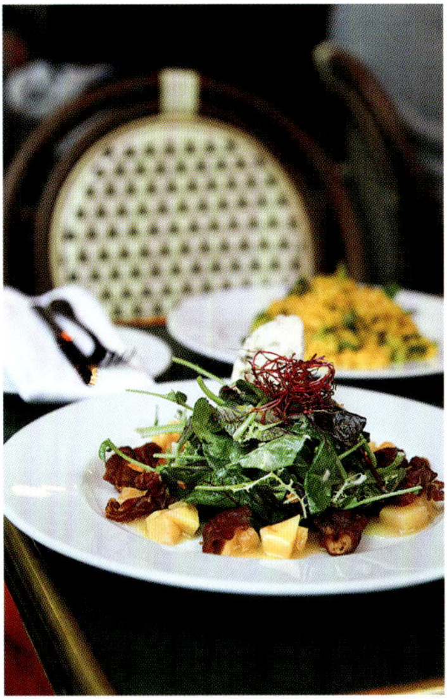

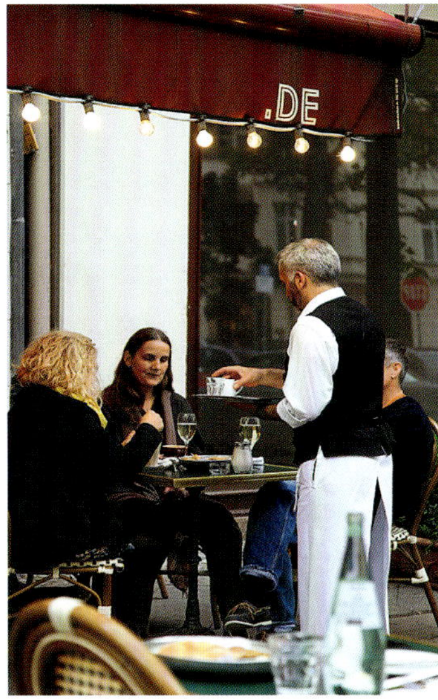

.DE

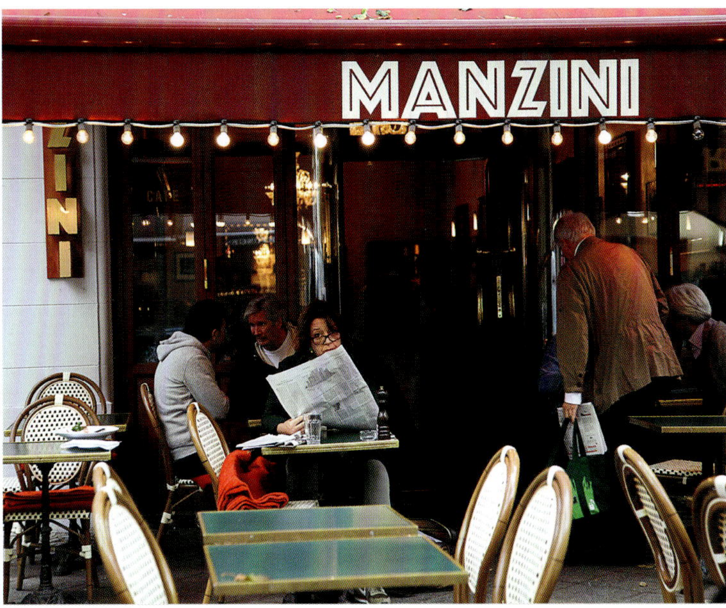

MANZINI
ZINI

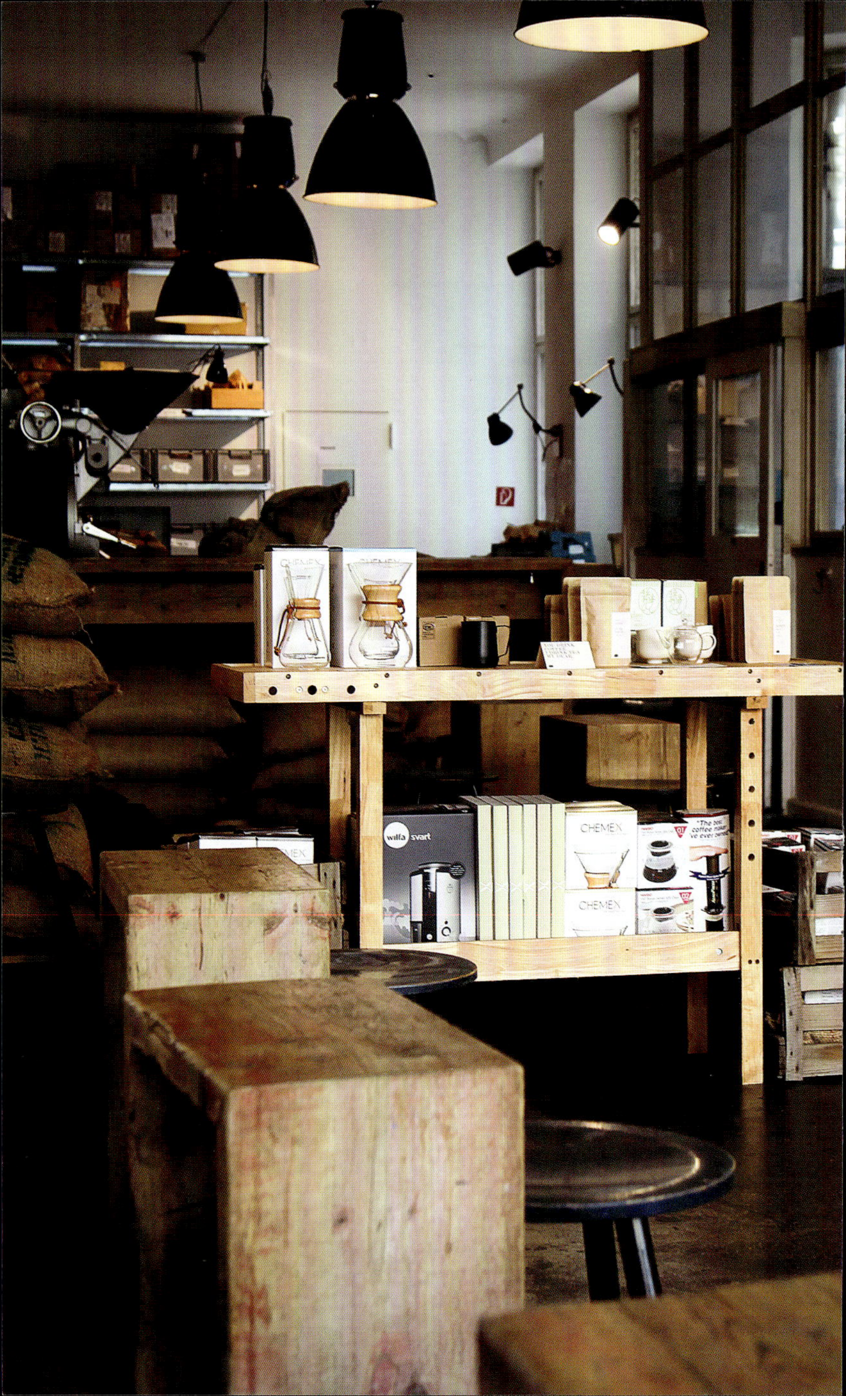
CHEMEX
CHEMEX
wilfa svart
CHEMEX
CHEMEX

Hotel Restaurant Café Bar Shop // Interview Interesting facts Recipe

THE BARN
COFFEE ROASTERS

THE BARN ROASTERY

Sugar and soya milk are off the menu at the Barn Roastery. Ralf Rüller, who runs this coffee shop with its own roastery, has made it his mission to create a hub for coffee lovers. That means being disciplined. Coffee available here is only made how it tastes best – and the owner's philosophy is strictly no sugar or soya milk. Soya milk has a too intense flavour – and sugar ...? No comment. A very limited selection of sandwiches and cakes also mirrors the regime, as the food must go with the coffee. These rules may be too strict for many people, but the true coffee aficionado has found the right address. Nowhere else in Mitte does the coffee taste so fresh, strong and pure.

If you still need a shot of soya milk or sugar, then try The Barn in Auguststraße – Ralf Rüller's first coffee shop. The rules aren't as strict in this tiny shop – which gets particularly crowded just after midday, when the agency workers arrive for an espresso after lunch – and the coffee is just as good. The interiors in both cafés are plain with plenty of wood and simple stools: barn style.

The Barn Roastery Address: Schönhauser Allee 8, Prenzlauer Berg
Website: www.thebarn.de Opening hours: Monday – Thursday 08:30 a.m. – 5 p.m., Friday 08:30 a.m. – 6 p.m., Saturday and Sunday 10 a.m. – 6 p.m.

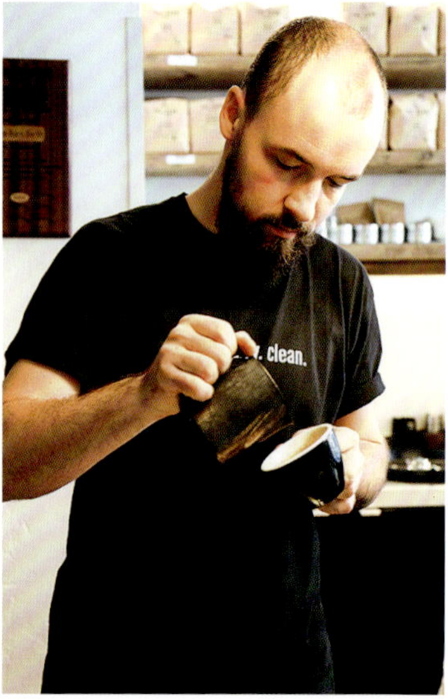
clean.

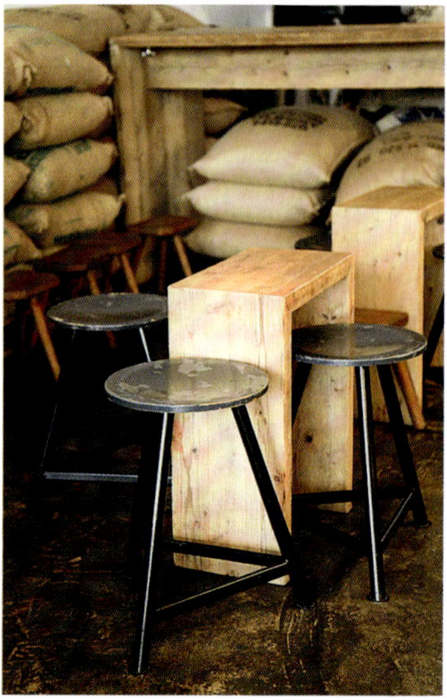

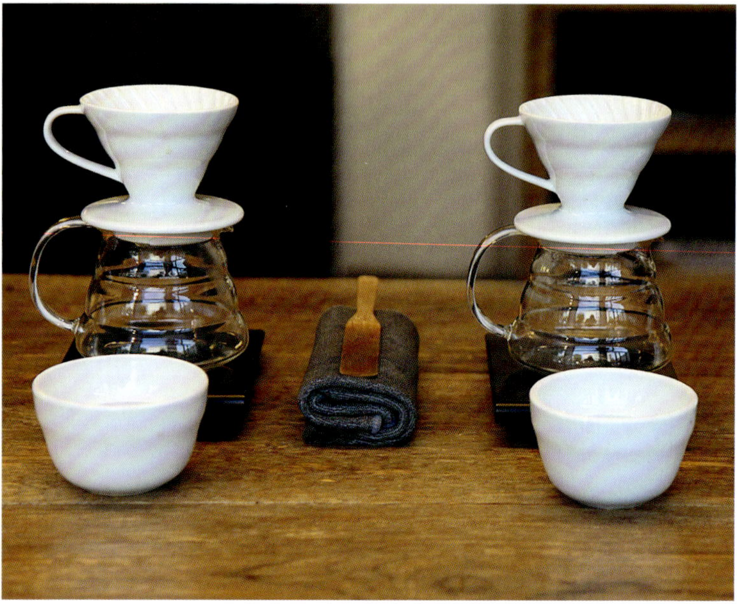

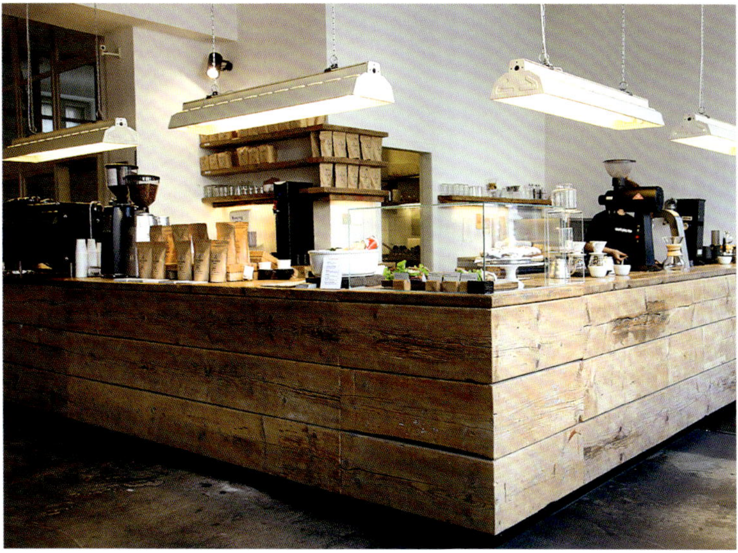

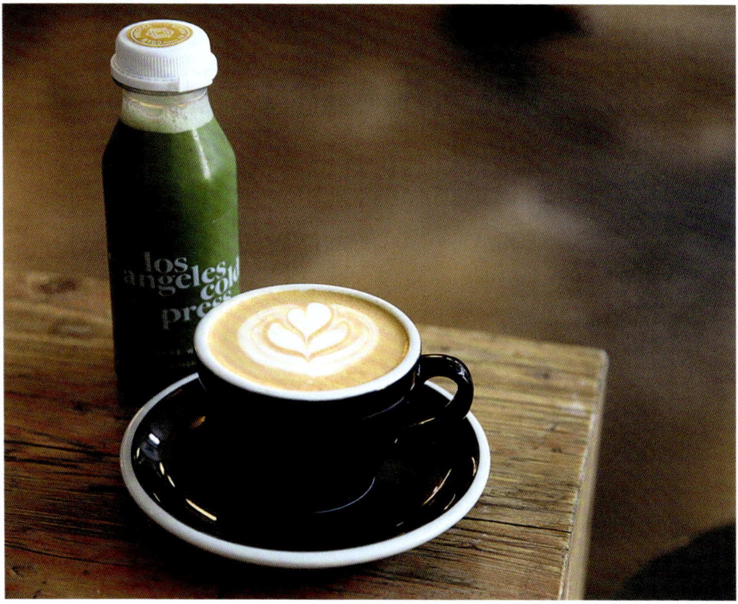
los
angeles
cold
press

Hotel Restaurant *Café* Bar Shop // Interview *Interesting facts* Recipe

☞ What do you fancy love?!

'What do you fancy love?' – a coffee bar in Charlottenburg – is a real gem. It's reminiscent of coffee shops in Los Angeles or New York, and fills a gap in West Berlin. It's well worth a visit just to sample the delicious cake, and the coffee is fantastic too. But the smoothies are the unique selling point – they are undoubtedly the best, most delicious and freshest anywhere in West Berlin.

Address: Knesebeckstraße 68/69, Charlottenburg
Website: www.whatdoyoufancylove.de
Opening hours: Monday – Friday 8 a.m. – 6 p.m.,
Saturday 9 a.m. – 6 p.m. and Sunday 10 a.m. – 6 p.m.

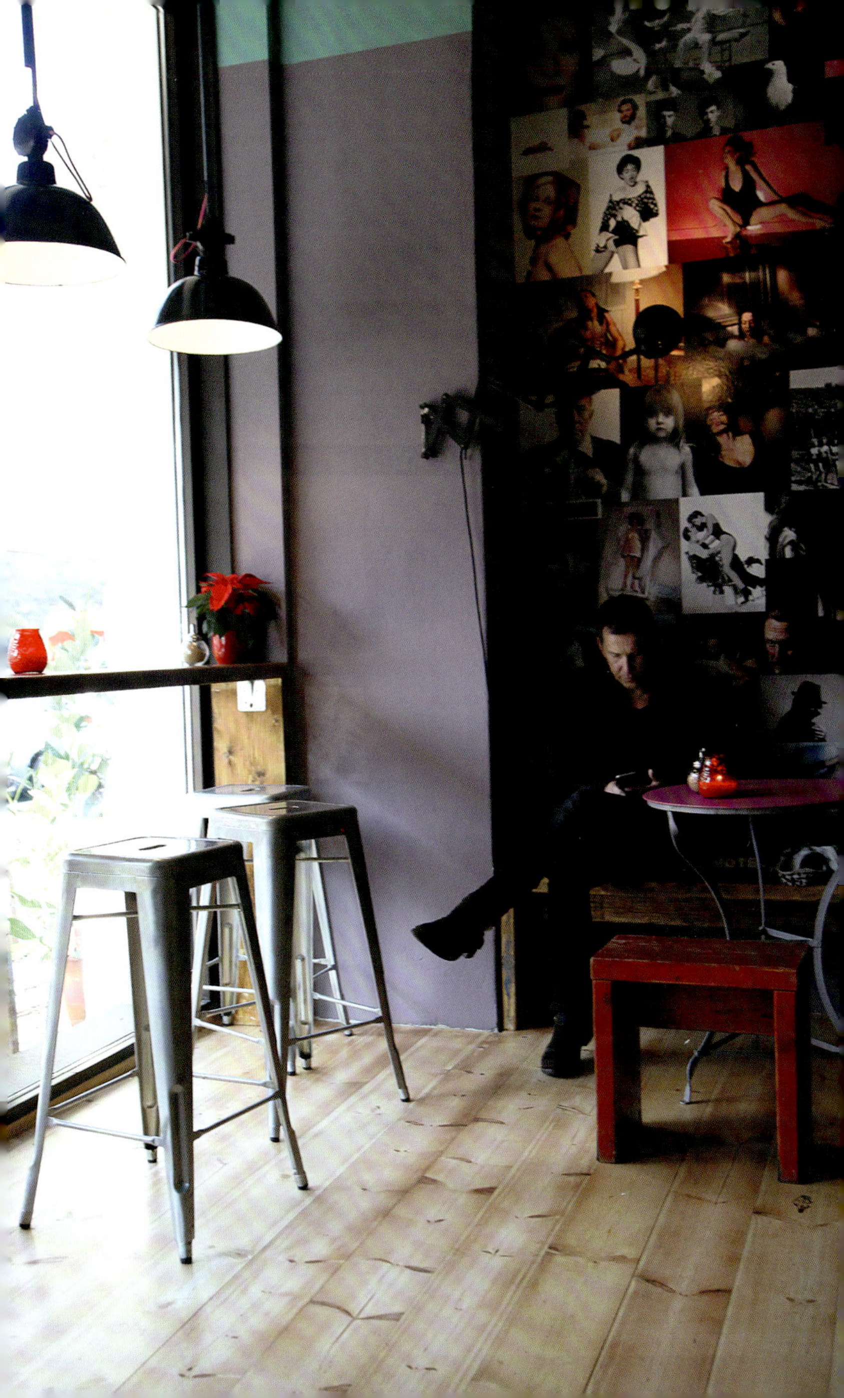

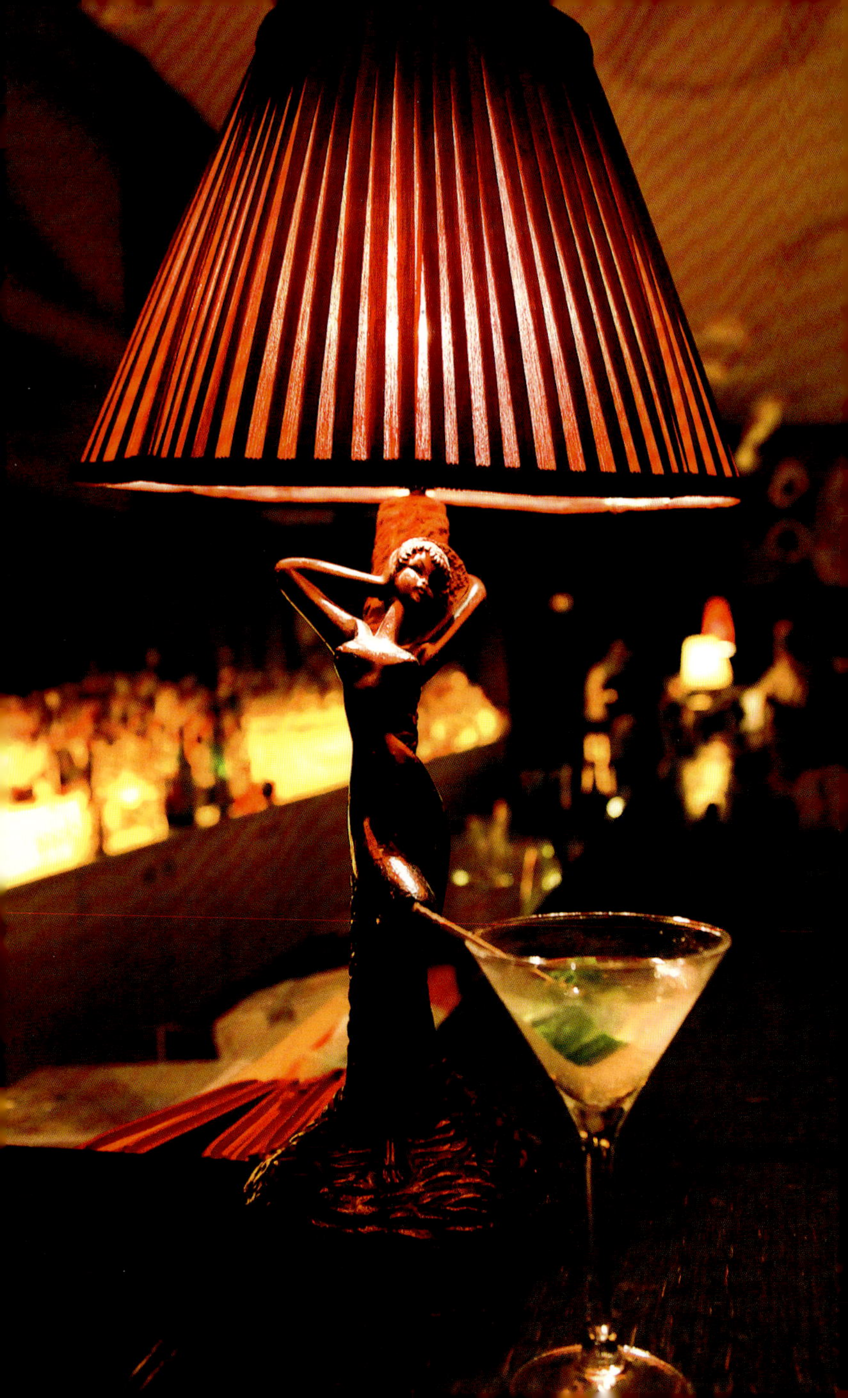

Hotel   Restaurant   Café   Bar   Shop   //   Interview   Interesting facts   Recipe

VICTORIA BAR

Just drop in. Don't be shy – apart from tourist parties, they let in all kinds of affable individuals here. Including the over-35s. An eclectic bunch of colourful people from all walks of life meet here, and fortunately ordinary drinkers, too. It opened in 2001 and now this classically modern bar is here to stay. A bar like Victoria Bar is hard to come by, as we've often searched unsuccessfully in other cities. So what's the secret of a good bar? Obviously, it's about the managers and their team. From the outset the committed bartenders contributed their boundless energy and wit: Beate Hindermann, blonde, likes wearing her hair in a pony-tail; Hermann Halkim, always dons his cap and owner Stefan Weber, who is tall and lanky. They've all been involved in Berlin's bar scene for decades. Stefan Weber is a passionate advocate of the world's traditional big bars; his ideas set the trend down to the bartenders' stylish outfits. The interiors are carefully designed with a sophisticated touch thanks to contemporary artworks decorating the walls. The cocktail menu offers classics as well as the bar's own inventions, so it takes time to choose. Whatever your favourite cocktail, it will definitely have the wow factor! Stefan's initial plan was to establish a hotel bar offering club sandwiches and roast beef like in the heyday of American cocktail culture, and he successfully achieved this in 2006.

Victoria Bar   Address: Potsdamer Straße 102, Tiergarten
Phone: 0049 (0)30 25759977   Website: www.victoriabar.de   Opening hours:
Sunday – Thursday 6:30 p.m. – 3 a.m., Friday and Saturday 6:30 p.m. – 4 a.m.
Happy hour: Monday – Saturday 6:30 p.m. – 9:30 p.m., Sunday all night long

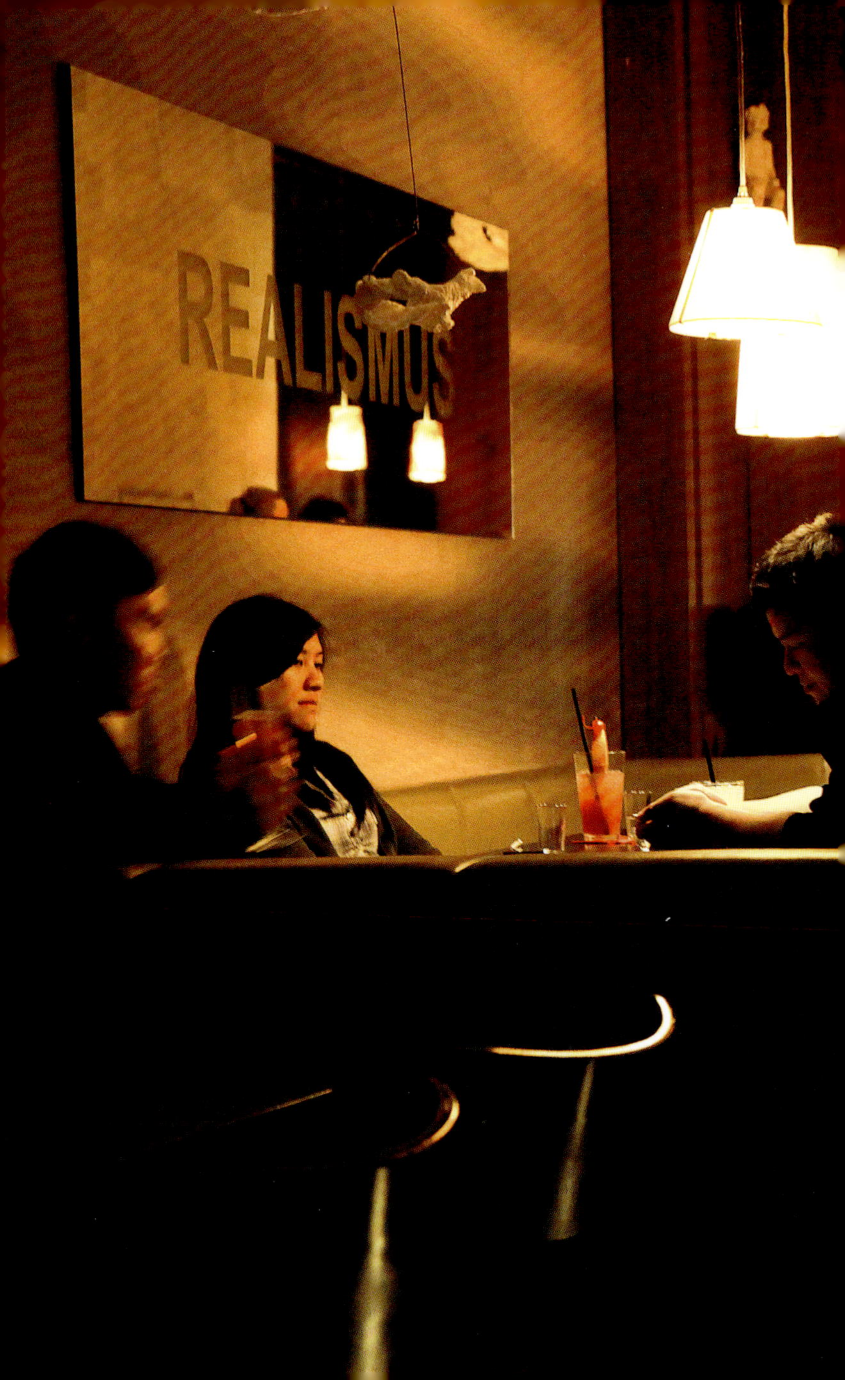
REALISMUS

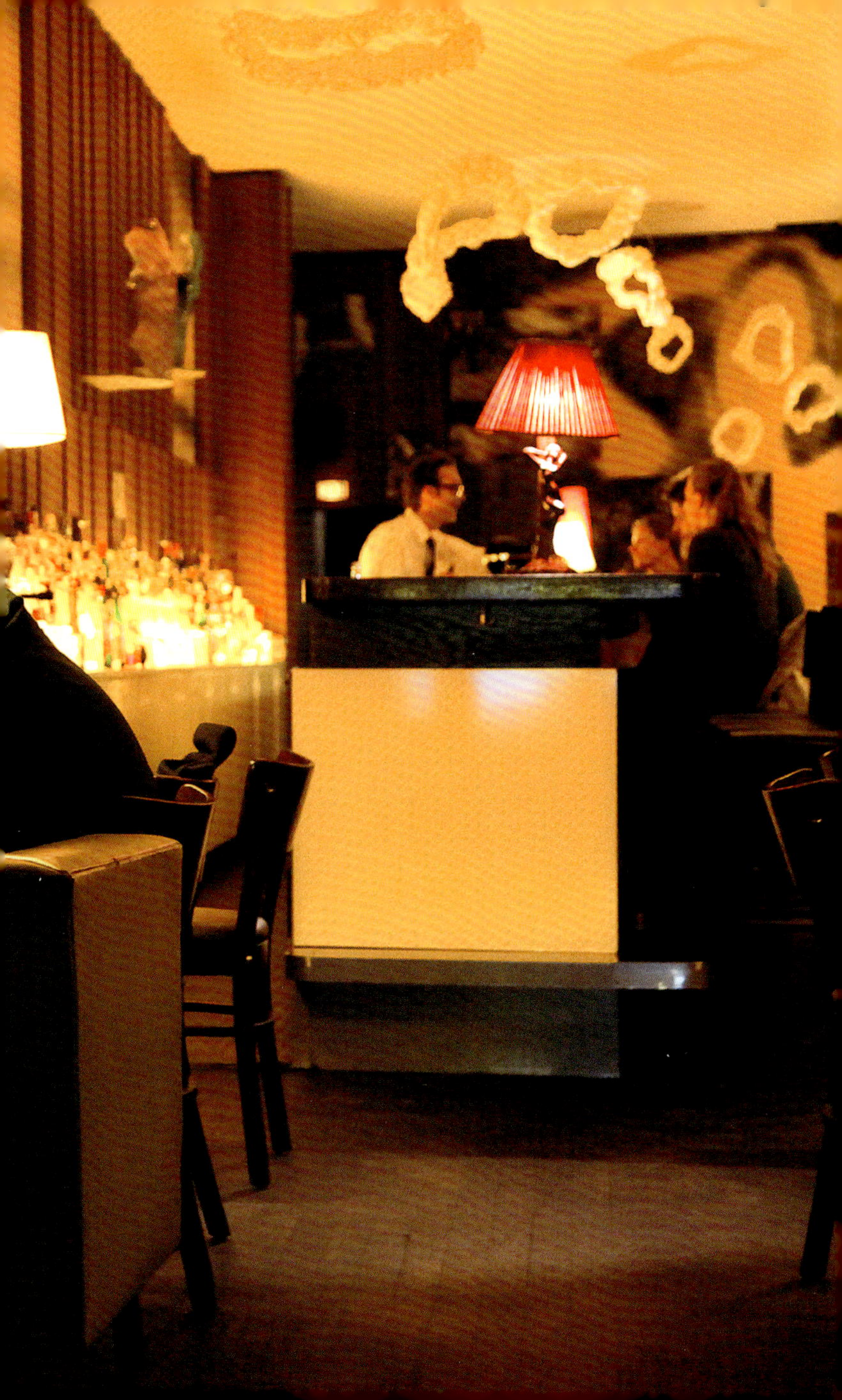

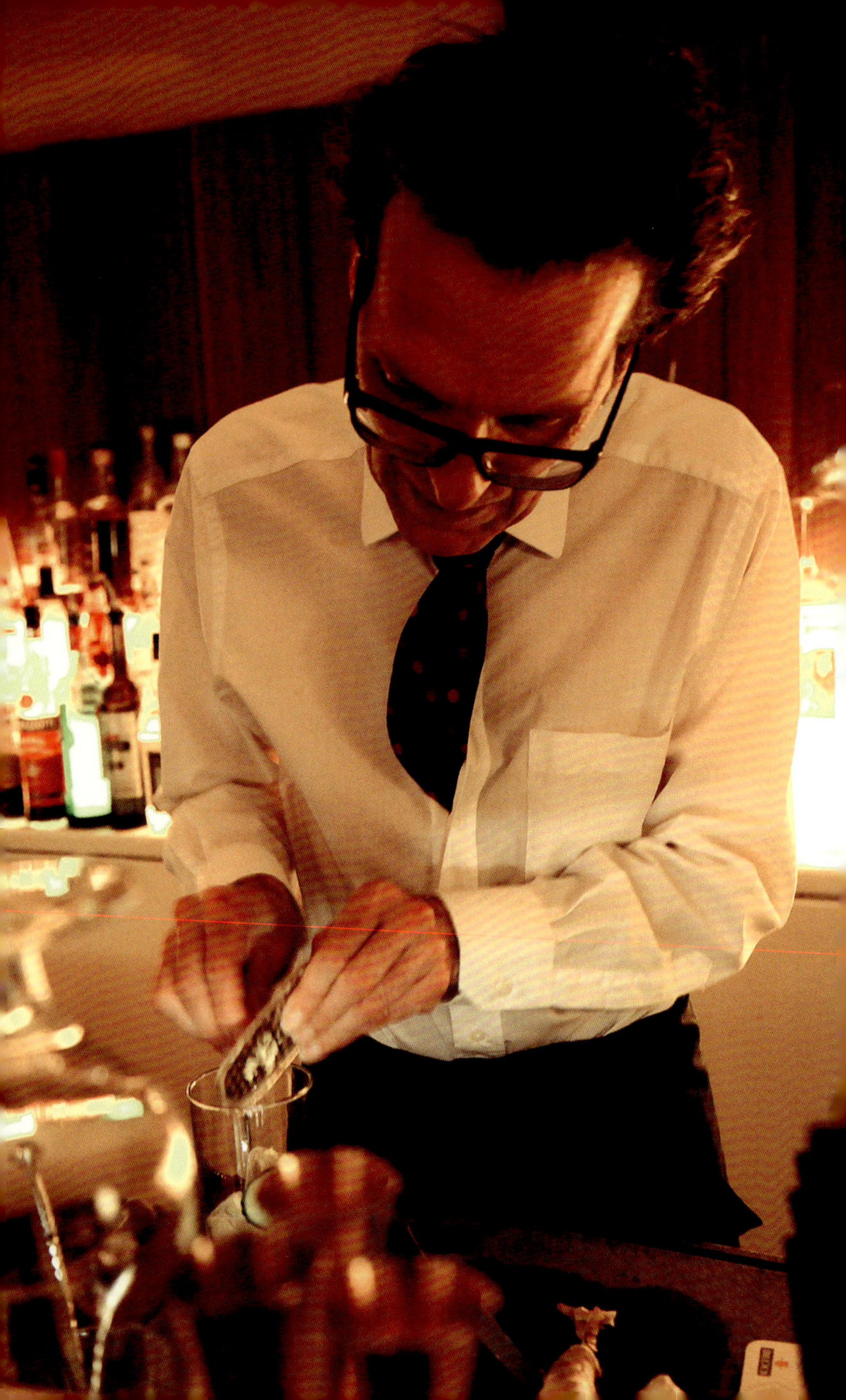

Hotel   Restaurant   Café   Bar   Shop   //   Interview   Interesting facts   Recipe

An interview with Stefan Weber
Owner and bartender

What motivated you to establish a bar in this locality?
This area wasn't easy at the start, but I still believed in it because of its central position. People who travel to dine out between Berlin Mitte and Charlottenburg stop off here later on. Potsdamer Strasse with all the little side streets has been a traditional district for nightlife even before the fall of the Wall, and now it's become the gallery quarter. After the vernissages and finissages the artists and gallery owners meet up at Victoria Bar.

A bar with contemporary artworks covering the walls. Are you a collector?
Art is one of my passions. That's why I invite contemporary artists to interpret the bar by contributing a work and presenting it. Works hanging on these walls include those by Martin Kippenberger, Marcel Dzarma, Douglas Gordon, Dieter Roth and Daniel Richter.

Which drink most disappoints you?
A Piña Colada doesn't exactly prove that you're a connoisseur. But if anyone wants one, they can also order this at our bar.

Which drink is en vogue right now?
Negroni, Old Fashioned and Pisco Sour.

What is your favourite cocktail at the moment?
The Pick Me Up, a champagne drink with Cognac, grenadine, lemon and Angostura.

In 2014 you celebrated a 13th anniversary and you still love your job?
Yes, I can't wait for the evening to begin when I'm on my way here.

BIER & SOFTDRINKS
CAFÉ
ESPRESSO
ESPRESSO MACCHIATO
AUSGABE

Hotel Restaurant Café Bar Shop // Interview Interesting facts Recipe

MARKT HALLE NEUN

MARKTHALLE NEUN

Markthalle Neun in Berlin Kreuzberg dates back to 1891 when it was first opened. It was one of the three remaining buildings of Berlin's original fourteen historic market halls. Until the 1970s, it was a popular meeting place and shopping centre. In the late 1970s Aldi, Kik and Drospa bought into the market hall, managing lots of small vendors and heralding the start of the demise.

Fast forward to 2009 and new life has been breathed into these walls. An initiative was set up firstly to revitalise the historic market hall and secondly to demonstrate the future of 'alternative shopping'. Now, regional and seasonal products with low food miles are on sale here.

Small-scale grocers can set out their stalls again. The weekly market is held every Tuesday, Friday and Saturday. In addition to various stalls there is an artisan bakery, a fish and meat smoking house, a microbrewery and a canteen where people can relax after shopping. Many of the locals enjoy a glass of white wine with their neighbours after shopping on Saturdays or they meet for lunch. Various events supplement the weekly market, for example, Street Food Thursday or the breakfast club.

Markthalle Neun Address: Eisenbahnstraße 42/43, Kreuzberg
Phone: 0049 (0)30 61073473 Werbsite: www.markthalleneun.de
Opening hours: Weekly market: Tuesdays and Fridays noon – 8 p.m.,
Saturdays 10 a.m. – 6 p.m.

-86-

Hotel   Restaurant   Café   Bar   Shop   //   Interview   Interesting facts   Recipe

☞ Street Food Thursday

The absolute highlight at Markhalle Neun is Street Food Thursday. Every Thursday the market hall turns into a paradise for all those 'foodies' without their own restaurant and start-up funding, yet with grand ambitions to follow their passion: cooking! And that means: British pies, Thai tapioca dumplings, Mexican tacos, Allgäuer Kässpatzen (cheese noodles), Peruvian ceviche, Nigerian fufu and Korean buns. That's not forgetting the big crowd of international style gurus aged 20 to 40, plus the unlimited wine.

Opening hours: Every Thursday 5 p.m. – 10 p.m.

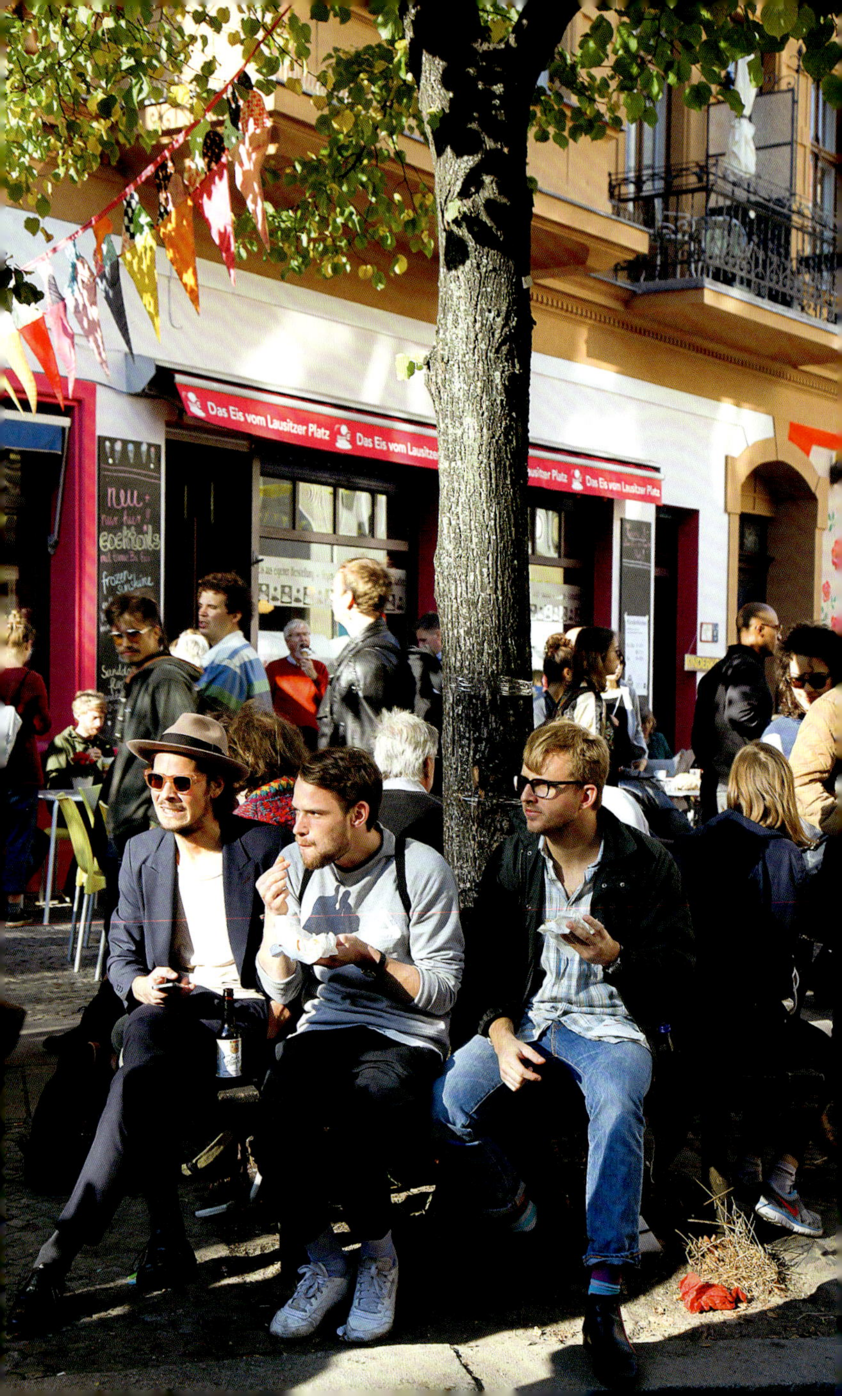
Das Eis vom Lausitzer Platz
Das Eis vom Lausitzer Platz

SMART TRAVELLING

GOOD TO KNOW

Berlin is a big place, so we've kept this information section small. Instead of listing anything and everything, we've focussed on giving you the right tips for a perfect weekend break: interesting facts about the way of life in Berlin and a small, hand-picked selection of sights, walks and recommendations for Sunday activities. We've also included a handy map with all of our favourite spots to help you get your bearings right away and make the most of your time in Berlin..

BERLIN DIALECT

Berliners can be amazingly direct and this takes time to get used to. Berlin dialect sounds more openly working class than other accents. Berlin schools therefore strictly prohibited the local dialect in the classroom. In the West the educated middle class rarely spoke Berlinese; they only reverted to it if they experienced an attack of road rage! After the fall of the Berlin Wall, the mélange of local dialects changed because in the East everybody – from professors to shop assistants – relied on colloquialisms without inhibitions. Speaking Berlinese is like putting on a coat of armour – that's why the local vernacular is so popular in inner-city traffic! Words like *Schnauze* (gob), *Atze* (bro or dude) or *icke* (I or me) are shoved under your nose like sticks of dynamite. And they omit the

R in the end: *Biste och Balina?* which translates as, 'Are you a Berliner as well?' A typical scene in a Berlin bus is when a passenger obligingly shows the bus driver their ticket, and the driver retorts, *Soll ick rinbeeßen oder wat?*, and a rough translation is, 'What am I supposed to do with that? Eat it?'

Food

Berlina Weiße	White beer with syrup
Blondes	Berlin wheat beer
Bollen	onions
Bollenpiepen	leek
Bulette	meatballs
Fressalien	food
Järtnerwurst	cucumber
Joldbroiler	chicken
Knüppl	long bread roll
Molle	a glass of beer
Ostseeforelle	salted herring
Pappdiskus	pizza
Schrippe	bread roll
Schrippnarchitekt	baker
Schustajunge	dark bread roll
Sturmsack	cream puff
Untaseeboot	herring

Daily routine

dufte	excellent
einpfeifen	eating
een paar Zerquetschte	a few cents
icke	I or me
Knökn, Kohle, Penunse, Pinke, Schotta, Zasta	terms denoting 'money'
Mischpoke	riffraff – family (negative connotation)
piekfein	very posh, dressed up
urst	superlative form of expression, e.g. 'totally', 'well'
wa	a tag question at the end of the sentence, e.g. Is' aba warm heute, wa? ('It's warm today, isn't it?').

People

Atze	bro, dude, man, buddy
Ick wa' janz baff	I was astonished
erschossen sein	to be exhausted
falscher Fuffziger	dishonest person
Fatzke	vain, arrogant individual
Ische	girlfriend, wife
jewieft	smart, streetwise
knast haben	to feel hungry
olle Schachtel	old or ugly lady
schnabulieren	to eat or munch
uffmucken	contradict
veräppeln	to pull somebody's leg

Local terms

Istanbul-Express	Underground line 7 between Spandau and Schlesisches Tor
jwd	janz weit draußen – 'very far outside town' or peripheral Berlin district
Kaff	provincial city
Potse	Potsdamer Strasse

BERLINERS

How do you spot a genuine Berliner? An instant giveaway will be the familiar challenge, 'Where do you really come from?' Berliners are proud of their heritage, which often creates an uneasy air of exclusivity. Newcomers prefer to become Berliners quickly to avoid being seen as outsiders and experiencing an awkward feeling of isolation. Luckily, there are some signs of improvement. However, Berliners often stand out because of what they wear: their trademark look is unkempt with creased shirts and their outfits reflect anything but the latest fashions. Berliners love browsing in vintage shops where their purchases are measured by weight. Retailers probably have the worst time here than anywhere else in Germany. The idea of 'normal clothing' is taken to the extreme. All those who feel the urge to try out a quirky new style should do so during this trip, as in Berlin you are bound to attract more attention in smart, contemporary designer wear. Remember that you'll soon feel overdressed in Berlin.

CONTRASTING ARCHITECTURE

Berlin is striking not so much thanks to its architectural coherence like Barcelona, nor for its volume of antiquities like Rome. It has no picturesque old quarter like Vienna. Rather, Berlin is more a spatial haven where the buildings have landed after emerging from different time zones and societal systems. In the East you stumble upon Alexanderplatz as a model of socialist architecture and pass socialist slab-concrete apartment complexes leading to Karl-Marx-Allee – a testament to Communist monumental architecture par excellence. At the same time, on Torstrasse, Roger Bundschuh created the spectacular grey L40 concrete condominium building. Graft architects developed the idiosyncratic Tor149 structure, while not far from the former site of the Berlin Wall, at Chausseestrasse, Daniel Libeskind developed his first Berlin residential building called Sapphire. Beautifully restored inner courtyards in Berlin Mitte and Prenzlauer Berg evoke a pre-industrial age and the city's rich Jewish cultural heritage, while at Potsdamer Platz ultra modern skyscrapers herald a contemporary age. The futuristic Chancellery building is close to the majestic boulevard Unter den Linden the historic origins of which are still discernible en route for the Museum Island and its treasure collections. The buildings along Kurfürstendamm in the West hint at decadent consumption. Nearby Charlottenburg Palace was the residence of the Hohenzollern dynasty for 300 years. Whichever direction you turn in Berlin, around every corner you'll witness the contrasting legacies of a turbulent history and a new city-in-the-making.

Well-organized architectural guided tours are available at
www.ticket-b.de
www.guiding-architects.net

ART HIGHLIGHTS

Museum Island

The unique group of buildings and cultural amenities near the boulevard Unter den Linden ranges from the classicist Altes Museum (antiquities collection) with its pleasure garden, the Alte Nationalgalerie (19th century art, including Monet and Renoir), Bode Museum (art from the Byzantine period up to the 18th century) and the Pergamonmuseum (archaeological finds from antiquity, the Ancient Near East and Islamic art) with its world-famous Pergamon Altar – please note that this is closed until 2016 for building works.

A real highlight is the Neue Museum, with the Egyptian Museum and bust of Queen Nofretete. The building stood in ruins for 60 years after the Second World War. Star architect David Chipperfield transformed the building to its former simplicity and splendour, while retaining its unique character. Throughout the museum, the British architect has made it clear where he restored the late classical structure of the 1856 landmark building, and where he complemented the architecture and wall paintings. Touring the rooms is an amazing experience of old juxtaposed with new. It's best to book your ticket online because the museum is extremely popular.

www.museumsinsel-berlin.de

Neues Museum
Bodestraße 1-3, Mitte
Phone: 0049 (0)30 266424242
www.neues-museum.de
Daily 10 a.m. – 6 p.m.
Thursday to 8 p.m.

For all those interested in contemporary art, a visit to the temporary exhibitions at the Martin-Gropius-Bau is a must – there are photography shows as well as spectacular installations by Ólafur Elíasson and an original Viking ship. Visit the Hamburger Bahnhof (the old Berlin–Hamburg railway terminus) to see more contemporary art collections like the Friedrich Christian Flick Collection or the Marx Collection. This gallery presents art trends from the 1960s to the present-day and includes works by Andy Warhol, Joseph Beuys, Keith Haring, Anselm Kiefer and Gerhard Richter. Unfortunately, the Neue Nationalgalerie, located in Mies van der Rohe's landmark classical modernist building, is closed for refurbishment until 2018.

Martin-Gropius-Bau
Niederkirchnerstraße 7, Kreuzberg
Phone: 0049 (0)30 254860
www.gropiusbau.de
Wednesday – Monday 10 a.m. – 7 p.m.

Hamburger Bahnhof
Invalidenstraße 50-51, Tiergarten

Phone: 0049 (0)30 39783411
www.hamburgerbahnhof.de
Tuesday, Wednesday, Friday
10 a.m. – 6 p.m., Thursday
10 a.m. – 8 p.m., Saturday and
Sunday 11 a.m. – 6 p.m.

Jewish Museum
A visit to Europe's largest Jewish Museum not just because of its exhibitions, but also to encounter its architecture. Daniel Libeskind, himself the son of Holocaust survivors, created a new, zig-zag shaped building whose concrete walls, oblique axes and jagged angles are a sensory experience culminating in the Garden of Exile. The sloping floors and concrete stelae on a gradient are intentional – in Libeskind's words 'to completely disorient the visitor' – and to acquaint the public with the feeling of the diaspora.

Lindenstraße 9-14, Kreuzberg
Phone: 0049 (0)30 25993300
www.jmberlin.de
Monday 10 a.m. – 10 p.m., Tuesday to Sunday 10 a.m. – 8 p.m.

Holocaust Memorial
Between the Brandenburg Gate and Potsdamer Platz, 2,700 grey-black concrete stelae of the Memorial to the Murdered Jews of Europe rise up into the sky. This memorial caused heated political controversy in the planning phase. It invites you to walk among the field of concrete pillars, get away from the hubbub of the city and meander in-between the rows of stelae, which vary in height up to four metres, past tightly packed concrete columns towards the middle of the uneven, sloping site. Architect Peter Eisenman's intention was for the visitor to become immersed, to vanish and become totally self-reliant. His appeal is for analysis and reflection, and at the same time he focuses on the process of commemoration.

Adjacent to the memorial and below the field of concrete stelae is an underground Information Centre. The exhibition here traces the personal histories of persecuted Jews, with educational information about their deprivation of rights, persecution and murder.

Information Centre
Cora-Berliner-Straße 1, Tiergarten
Phone: 0049 (0)30 26394336
www.stiftung-denkmal.de
Tuesday – Sunday 10 a.m. – 8 p.m.

C|O Berlin

In a prime location at Bahnhof Zoo railway station, adjacent to the Zoo Palast cinema and the Bikini building, the photography exhibition centre opened its doors in late 2014. Works by Annie Leibovitz, Peter Lindbergh, René Burri, Martin Parr and other top photographers are on display. Lectures, discussions and workshops are also held here. The gallery is located in Amerika Haus, a 1957 modernist building. The café is welcoming and there is a large bookshop.

Hardenbergstraße 22, Charlottenburg
Phone: 0049 (0)30 28444160
www.co-berlin.org
Daily 11 a.m. – 8 p.m.

Art in Mitte

Auguststraße used to be the epicentre of Berlin's art world. Kunst-Werke, Institute for Contemporary Art is still a top address today. The KW Institute is home to the Berlin Biennale film showcase and contemporary group shows. It also accommodates Café Bravo which is ideal for delicious snacks; the glass building designed by artist Dan Graham also has a pleasant courtyard garden.

A few buildings further away: Galerie Eigen + Art that made Neo Rauch and Leipzig art world famous. The me Collectors Room established by Thomas Olbricht is a newcomer as of 2010. At first, this art collection was critically received because of its ostentatious and invasive building that protrudes into the street like a foreign object. Now, however, it fits in well. On display are curiosities from the 17th century as well as Warhol icons and contemporary art – a veritable conglomeration of art and objets d'art and temporary exhibitions. You can also stop at the café for a coffee or lunch at the long oak table.

KW

Kunst-Werke
Auguststraße 69, Mitte
Phone: 0049 (0)30 2434590
www.kw-berlin.de
Wednesday – Monday noon – 7 p.m.
Thursday noon – 9 p.m.

Eigen + Art
Auguststraße 26, Mitte
Phone: 0049 (0)30 2806605

www.eigen-art.com
Tuesday – Saturday 11 a.m. – 6 p.m.

me Collectors Room
Auguststraße 68, Mitte
Phone: 0049 (0)30 86008510
www.me-berlin.com
Tuesday – Sunday noon – 6 p.m.

Boros Collection
A former Imperial bunker right at the heart of the city is home to the private art collection of Christian and Karen Boros. The art collector family lives in a glass penthouse built on the roof. This inspirational collection comprises 130 artworks by 22 artists, many of whom personally installed their works. The collection is displayed on five floors – astronomical pictures by Thomas Ruff, a six-metre high, newly constructed swamp tree by Ai Weiwei, an installation by Tomás Saraceno, who strings up cables like a giant spider's web through the room, while Ólafur Eliasson brings the city inside the bunker. The young Berlin artist duo, Manon Awst and Benjamin Walther, also make visitors clamber over metal pipes.

At sammlung-boros.de you can register for a guided tour. The tours are available on Fridays, Saturdays and Sundays and take approximately 1.5 hours.
Tip: Book early because the collection is extremely popular.

Reinhardtstraße 20, Mitte
Phone: 0049 (0)30 27594065 or 0049 (0)30 240833300
www.sammlung-boros.de

Autocenter
A glance at the Autocenter website is always worthwhile. The Space for Contemporary Art founded by Maik Schierloh and Joep van Liefland presents the city's most enthralling exhibitions. Berlin's art scene shares this view – and transforms every launch into a hip event.

Leipziger Straße 56, Mitte
www.autocenterart.de

Tip: Bauhaus tours are highly recommended. These are organized by the Bauhaus-Archiv and Museum für Gestaltung (www.bauhaus.de) in conjunction with art:berlin.

www.artberlin-online.de

GALLERY WALKING TOURS

Starting point: Alexanderplatz

... from here it's a must to experience the atmosphere of bygone 'actually existing Socialism'. This was represented in all its glory at Karl-Marx-Allee and Strausberger Platz.

From Alexanderplatz turn straight into Karl-Marx-Allee and, on the left-hand side, you will notice the legendary Kino International cinema (Karl-Marx-Allee 33). This modern building opened in 1963 with the premiere of the Soviet revolutionary drama 'Optimistic Tragedy'. Its GDR crystal chandeliers, spectacular panoramic windows, golden curtain and elegant Socialist charm still make stars like Patti Smith or Michel Gondry awestruck whenever they are in the city to promote their films at the Berlinale International Film Festival.

Bar Babette (Karl-Marx-Allee 36) is just across the road. In this glass cube building, which was a former beauty salon and has now been turned into a hip bar, the customers enjoy 1960s retro styling. They take their seats on synthetic leather benches at small tables, or in summer sit outdoors on the pavement with a perfect view of the 'Alex'.

On the other side, in the modernist glass cube – in GDR days this was an artisan handcraft shop – Galerie Capitain Petzel has now established itself (Karl-Marx-Allee 45). International art trends and top names are showcased in these premises that are worth seeing just for the architecture.

Only a few steps away you arrive at Strausberger Platz where in best Stalinist 'confectionary' architectural style (similar to art deco) and surrounded by the famous Floating Ring Fountain (Schwebender Ring) a number of galleries have been established: Jette Rudolph (Strausberger Platz 4) and Wagner + Partner (Strausberger Platz 8). This is the ideal place to survey architect Hermann Henselmann's opulent 'confectionery' buildings.

It's worth taking a stroll up the former Stalinallee – much wider than the Champs-Elysee – as far as Strasse der Pariser Kommune to the Karl-Marx-Buchhandlung (a book shop, which was an old GDR institution and made famous by the Oscar-winning film The Lives of Others). Several agencies now have their head offices here. Directly adjacent is gallery Peres Projects (Karl-Marx-Allee 82) fresh from Los Angeles and boasting James Franco on its list of artists.

From the Neue Nationalgalerie

... as this is closed for refurbishment until 2018, you can only admire the Mies van der Rohe building from the outside. From here, you arrive in what is currently Berlin's art district. More than 300 galleries make this city a paradise for contemporary art lovers. In recent years some of the most interesting galleries have relocated here to the former premises of Der Tagesspiegel, rear courtyards, ex-businesses and elegant old apartment buildings.

At Schöneberger Ufer head for Galerie Esther Schipper (Schöneberger Ufer 65) – the city's leading gallery and one of the most important international galleries. Wien Lukatsch is in the floor above, while Isabella Bortolozzi (Schöneberger Ufer 61) and Aurel Scheibler (Schöneberger Ufer 71) are all located nearby.

Then turn into Potsdamer Straße where several galleries have set up in the old Tagesspiegel premises (Potsdamer Straße 77-87). Among them are Arratia Beer, whose programme includes Omer Fast and Matthew Metzger, as well as Galerie Guido W. Baudach, which set up after the fall of the Berlin Wall in the vacant building in Berlin Mitte and now represents artists like Thomas Zipp. Gallery Blain/Southern acts for artists such as Damien Hirst or Lucian Freud and Gallery Thomas Fischer or also Galeria Plan B., which specializes in the past 50 years of Romanian art.

These galleries are surrounded by Galerie Arndt (Potsdamer Straße 96), Galerie Cinzia Friedlaender (Potsdamer Straße 105), Galerie Judin (Potsdamer Straße 83) and many more that you will notice before turning into Kurfürstenstrasse. In her exhibitions, Tanya Leighton (Kurfürstenstraße 156) constantly tests the limits of genres from cinema and other disciplines. Supportico Lopez (Kurfürstenstraße 14b) from Naples showcases artists like Steve Bishop, while Sommer&Kohl (Kurfürstenstraße 13/14) presents installations by the magnificent Eva Berendes or Knut Henrik Henriksens.

The galleries are usually open from Tuesday to Saturday.

For a light snack afterwards, try the popular, traditional Austrian Café Einstein for your Verlängerten (black espresso served with extra hot water), Kaiserschmarrn (Austrian dessert pancake with raisins) or Wiener Schnitzel.

Kurfürstenstraße 58, Tiergarten
Phone: 0049 (0)30 26150916
www.cafeeinstein.com
Daily 9 a.m. – 1 a.m.

EINSTEIN

THEATRES – TOP CHOICES

Volksbühne
In 1992 Frank Castorf took over as director of this modern and monumental theatre building where actresses and actors like Sophie Rois or Martin Wuttke perform on stage in highly topical and controversial productions.

Linienstraße 227, Mitte
Phone: 0049 (0)30 240650
www.volksbuehne-berlin.de

Maxim Gorki Theater
With a new director and the city's youngest and most idiosyncratic ensemble, this small, state-funded theatre is also the most thrilling stage in Germany. Its cutting-edge productions give uncannily clear insights into social reality, and its premiere parties are unrivalled. Make a reservation – it's a must!

Am Festungsgraben 2, Mitte
Phone: 0049 (0)30 202210
www.gorki.de

Schaubühne
Nina Hoss and Lars Eidinger appear on stage here, directed by Falk Richter and Michael Thalheimer – and

you should keep an eye on the website for updates about the Autistic Disco with Eidinger at the mixing desk. Ignore the groupies idling at the DJ booth and hit the dance floor to sounds of the best dance music from Grandmaster Flash to Electro.

Kurfürstendamm 153, Wilmersdorf
Phone: 0049 (0)30 890020
www.schaubuehne.de

FESTIVALS

Various festivals and other events are held all year round.

The season gets off to a stylish start with Fashion Week in January. Although the shows and fairs are invitation only, the whole city comes alive with fashion hype. You can saunter from one pop-up store to the next. At Torstrasse there are also plenty of one-off shows and special events (the same applies for the autumn edition of Fashion Week in July).

www.mbfashionweek.com

The Berlinale International Film Festival is held in February. This is one of the biggest audience festivals worldwide. More than 400 films are incorporated into the programme that annually attracts about 325,000 film enthusiasts who are lured by the magic of the Berlinale. Tickets can be obtained online as well as at various advance box offices including the arcades at Potsdamer Platz. At the film premieres you can experience the electric atmosphere on the red carpet and see the stars close up.

www.berlinale.de

Gallery Weekend is a paradise for art lovers usually held in early May at venues across the city when numerous galleries open with special shows and exhibitions.

www.gallery-weekend-berlin.de

A fun attraction is the character art festival Pictoplasma and conference at the Babylon Cinema with public screenings every evening and an international audience. This is a celebration of monsters, stop motion, animation, graphic design and all kinds of characters, plus exhibitions at venues across the city and cool parties.

www.pictoplasma.com

The International Design-Festival DMY takes place in June. This is a vast exhibition held in an aircraft hangar of the disused airport at Tempelhof. It includes numerous small shows downtown, the official ceremony for the German Design Award as well as workshops, discussions and presentations from universities to international product designers.

DMY

www.dmy-berlin.com

In September, art galleries introduce their artists at the abc contemporary art event.

www.artberlincontemporary.com

TEMPELHOF AIRPORT

Is there another city where can you rollerskate and kitesurf on a former runway, hike over a vast meadow, and settle down in a brightly coloured, higgledy-piggledy community garden? Where else can you gaze far and wide as if overlooking open countryside and see as far as the iconic buildings of what once was Berlin's Tempelhof Airport? In 2014, a referendum was held to decide whether parts of this inner-city prime real estate should be redeveloped: local residents rejected the proposal. So now you can laze about on the grass, enjoy the sunset, do a fitness workout or test your balance on the central strip of the former runway.

The best access point is from Oderstrasse in Neukölln (underground/U-Bahn stop at Leinestrasse).

WHERE TO GO SHOPPING – AND WHAT TO BUY

Berlin has plenty of popular shopping centres that appeal to different groups. Our overview is intended to help you pinpoint the best locations and offers.

Mitte – around Alte/Neue Schönhauser Straße and Torstraße

Trend-setting youngsters love to shop in Mitte near the Hackescher Markt. All the mainstream brands are found at Alte and Neue Schönhauser Straße and Münzstraße. Smaller and more individual shops owned by Berlin designers and interesting concept stores are tucked away in the side streets – for example, blush, breathe, Type Design (Rosa-Luxemburg-Straße), Pro qm (Almstadtstraße), Wolfen, Do you read me?!, Petite Boutique (Auguststraße), Paper & Tea, Lala Berlin (Alte Schönhauser Str.), R.S.V.P. – Papier in Mitte, (Mulackstraße), Kaviar Gauche (Linienstraße), Soto, Stue and Lunette (Torstraße).

Mitte – around Friedrichstrasse

Wealthy and fashion-conscious shoppers gravitate to Gendarmenmarkt and Friedrichstraße. Quartier 206 is the centre – a mini luxury department store established by Anna Maria Jagdfeld. Designer brands like Gucci, Yves St. Laurent, Etro, La Perla and Louis Vuitton are located in the same block.

Quartier 206 DEPARTMENTSTORE

Galeries Lafayette department store is nearby and the popular concept store The Corner is at Gendarmenmarkt – three floors are dedicated to designers like Victor & Rolf, Balenciaga and Celine in addition to a selection of books and exclusive cosmetics. Occasional items of vintage furniture are available to purchase by negotiation.

Charlottenburg – Kudamm

Russians and stylish West Berliners go shopping along the Kurfürstendamm between Fasanenstraße and Leibnizstraße. With the exception of Zenker which offers the latest American labels, and the eclectic range at Uli Knecht, the line-up includes universally familiar brands such as Gucci, Jil Sander or Hermès.

Concept Mall in the listed Bikini building opposite the Memorial Church offers a shopping experience with German and international boutiques, concept and flagship stores, temporary pop-up shop booths and restaurants – the boutiques include Gestalten Pavillon, Vitra Shop, Closed, Aspesi, Andreas Murkudis and Mykita. The highlight is the huge panoramic window with a direct view of the monkeys' rock at Berlin Zoo and the 7,000 square metre spacious and leafy roof terrace.

Budapester Str. 42-50, Charlottenburg
Phone: 0049 (0)30 55496454
www.bikiniberlin.de
Monday – Saturday 10 a.m. – 8 p.m.

Charlottenburg – Savignyplatz
This is the shopping district for bona fide intellectuals and creative types. Some small, individual shops are still located on Bleibtreustraße, Mommsenstraße, Knesebeckstraße and Niebuhrstraße and towards Savignyplatz. The most interesting are Antonie Setzer, Bramigk & Breer, Adolph, Dopo Domani and Manufactum.

Kreuzberg
At Voo Concept Store – a former locksmith's shop situated in a rear courtyard on Oranienstraße – owned by the brothers Kaan and Yasin Müjdeci you can shop for the latest fashions from Acne, Wood Wood or Henry Vibskov. The store also stocks similarly exclusive accessories made by small labels and a selection of books and magazines. Round off the shopping trip with an excellent coffee from the Companion Coffee shop.

Voo Store Oranienstr. 24, Kreuzberg
Phone: 0049 (0)30 61651119
www.vooberlin.com
Monday – Saturday 11 a.m. – 8 p.m.

Schöneberg – Potsdamer Straße/
Winterfeldtplatz/Akazienstraße
Potsdamer Strasse 81 is a must for all fashionistas – at the former Tagesspiegel offices Andreas Murkudis has combined his four different shops from the rear courtyard at Münzstrasse under one roof. A concept store offering the latest and most desirable finds from the fashion, design and artworlds. Collections by Kostas Murkudis, Maison Martin Margiela and Dries van Noten appear alongside furniture from e15 and Nymphenburg porcelain.

A rendezvous for the enlightened. On Saturdays the market at Winterfeldtplatz is a popular meeting place for all Schöneberg residents, although people also flock here from other districts. From Goltzstraße via Akazienstraße as far as Hauptstraße, you'll find everything that an eco-conscious citizen needs: a well-stocked travel bookshop, small shops with tarot cards, crystals and Himalayan salt as well as appealing small delis offering excellent espresso, chocolate, wines and French specialities.

MARKETS

Kollwitz Farmers Market
Berlin's most popular market is at Kollwitzplatz in the heart of Prenzlauer Berg, surrounded by the facades of newly renovated buildings, as well as cafés, restaurants and small shops. This is a favourite meeting place for the hip crowd, young families and Kiez residents who come here to do their weekend shopping. There's a huge selection of seasonal gourmet delicacies, organic products, fresh fruit and vegetables from Brandenburg's market gardens. It's a good idea to arrive early to enjoy everything at a relaxed pace.

Kollwitzplatz, Prenzlauer Berg
Thursday noon – 7 p.m.
(Organic farmers market), Saturdays
10 a.m. – 4 p.m.

Organic market at Arkonaplatz
A small and charming local market in the Arkona-Kiez. This offers an exclusive selection of regional and organic products and mouthwatering snacks. The stalls selling grilled fish-on-a-stick and Belgian waffles are particularly popular.

Arkonaplatz, Mitte
Fridays noon – 7 p.m.

Winterfeldt market
Winterfeldt market is the westside's counterpart to Kollwitz farmers market.

Winterfeldtplatz, Schöneberg
Wednesdays and Saturdays
8 a.m. – 3 p.m.

Turkish market
For an authentic market atmosphere

visit 'Kreuzkölln'. The Turkish market on Maybachufer is buzzing with activity: on the right and left are stalls selling a huge variety of fruit and vegetables, delicious Turkish specialities and a vast array of fabrics. At the end of the market are a few stalls run by regional suppliers offering high quality organic products.

Maybachufer, Kreuzberg/Neukölln
www.tuerkenmarkt.de
Tuesdays and Fridays 11 a.m. – 6:30 p.m.

Organic market at Chamissoplatz
The organic market in the centre of Kreuzberg is at one of Berlin's prettiest squares evoking Parisian flair with its magnificent art nouveau buildings. Organically grown fruit and vegetables, plenty of herbs and speciality cheese and meats from the surrounding area are available here.

Chamissoplatz, Kreuzberg
www.oekomarkt-chamissoplatz.de
Saturdays 9 a.m. – 3 p.m.

Berlin Village Market Neue Heimat
This is a street food market run by the former managers of Bar25 with live music, DJs, bands and performances as well as stands and food trucks. In the evenings it morphs into an event with wine, cocktail and beer stands.

Revaler Straße 99 (Ecke Dirschauer Straße), Friedrichshain
www.neueheimat.com
Sunday noon – 10 p.m.
drinks served from 10 p.m.

Thai Meadow in Preußenpark
Whenever the sun shines on Sundays Preußenpark is transformed into a Thai Meadow – a market where the women spread plastic ground sheets over the grass, set up mini-stoves and prepare fresh traditional Thai food like chicken satay kebabs, fish balls, papaya salad and much more. Visitors can choose a spot to sit down on the grass and enjoy the gourmet delicacies. You can while away many hours here and try something from each seller. If it starts to get dark, you can order a Thai drink and watch the gambling.

Preußenpark, Wilmersdorf
Sundays in summer

PRINZESSINNENGARTEN

Since 2009 Prinzessinnengarten at Moritzplatz in Kreuzberg has been a green oasis with lush, thriving plants. This private garden initiative caused a stir worldwide and attracted many interested followers. You can learn all sorts here about vegetable and fruit cultivation, sustainability and harvesting or join a bee safari. In fine weather during the gardening season (April to October) you can enjoy a light bite every day at the garden café – of course, all the food served here is organic.

Prinzenstraße 35-38, Kreuzberg
Phone: 0049 (0)176 24332297
www.prinzessinnengarten.net

CHAMPION CURRYWURST

Berlin food is about simple, hearty fare with emphasis on rich and filling meals rather than refined taste. Berliners will find it hard to come up with examples of local dishes other than pork knuckle with pease pudding and eel in green sauce. Fortunately, in 1949 Herta Heuwer at the corner of Kant and Kaiser-Friedrich-Straße invented Currywurst – pork sausage prepared with a sweet and spicy sauce of tomato ketchup and 12 Indian spices (curry and cayenne pepper). The piquant sauce was poured over a boiled sausage seasoned with marjoram. Voilà! Mrs Heuwer had created the internationally popular and unique Berlin fast food hit. Her snack bar later moved to Stuttgarter Platz, where with up to 19 sales staff, she supplied famished customers with her original food, day and night. Kraft Foods made efforts to acquire the recipe and trademark rights, but Herta Heuwer declined. For the best Currywurst today, try these locations:

West: Biers 195
Kurfürstendamm 195, Charlottenburg
Phone: 0049 (0)30 8818942
Monday – Saturday 11 a.m. – 5 a.m.,
Sunday noon – 5 a.m.

East: Konnopke
Schönhauser Allee 44, Prenzlauer Berg
www.konnopke-imbiss.de
Monday – Friday 10 a.m. – 8 p.m.
Saturday noon – 8 p.m.

BERLIN OUTDOORS

The best thing after Berlin's harsh winter is to be able to sit outdoors again. The café owners cannot wait for the first rays of spring sunshine to set out their tables in the garden or on the pavement. Here are some tips for our favourite outdoor venues.

Prater

The Prater is Berlin's oldest and biggest authentic beer garden – this place attracts all kinds of visitors.

Kastanienallee 7–9, Prenzlauer Berg
Phone: 0049 (0)30 4485688
Monday –Friday from 6 p.m., Saturday and Sunday from noon, Beer garden:
April – September, daily from noon

Beach bar Mitte at Bode Museum

A beach haven at Monbijou park directly overlooks the majestic Bode Museum. The beach vibe is completed with real sand and traditional deck chairs. The beach bar supplies everyone with chilled drinks. Early evening is the best time to visit.

Monbijoupark, Bodestraße 1, Mitte
Phone: 0049 (0)30 20905555
www.strandbar-mitte.de
Daily from 10 a.m.

Café at the Neuer See

The café is located in a corner of Tiergarten park and well away from the hubbub of downtown Berlin. This café is always full with a lively atmosphere and an eclectic crowd of trend-setting visitors.

Lichtensteinallee 2, Tiergarten
Phone: 0049 (0)30 2544930
Daily 10 a.m. – 11 p.m.

Freischwimmer

For a brief moment you may imagine you're seated in a restaurant by a canal in Asia, but Freischwimmer is equally reminiscent of a café in the Kreuzberg Kiez. The terrace is built over the water and in sunny weather you can spend the entire day here listening to the splashing water. You can also hire the restaurant for private events.

Vor dem Schlesischen Tor 2A, Kreuzberg Phone: 0049 (0)30 61074309
www.freischwimmer-berlin.com
Monday – Friday noon – till late, Saturday and Sunday from 10 a.m.

BROWSING AT FLEA MARKETS

Enjoy a journey of discovery at the Sunday flea markets. The flea market at Arkona-Kiez in Mitte is small, personal and a favourite with the 'in-crowd'. All kinds of rummage and one-off vintage pieces are available here, plus the occasional object of nostalgia from GDR days. Arriving early will boost your chances of finding something special. If you haven't had enough, feel free to carry on browsing at the flea market at Mauerpark just a few streets away. Afterwards, bargain hunters can enjoy a coffee at Bonanza Coffee Roasters and admire their finds. Alternatively, they can continue the discovery tour at the flea market at Schöneberg city hall or at Boxhagener Platz in Friedrichshain.

Arkonaplatz, Mitte
Sunday 10 a.m. – 4 p.m.

Mauerpark
Bernauer Str. 63 – 64, Prenzlauer Berg
Sunday 8 a.m. – 6 p.m.

John-F.-Kennedy-Platz 1, Schöneberg
Saturday and Sunday 9 a.m. – 4 p.m.

Boxhagener Platz, Friedrichshain
Sunday 10 a.m. – 6 p.m.

Bonanza Coffee Roasters
Oderberger Str. 35, Prenzlauer Berg
www.bonanzacoffee.de
Monday – Friday 8:30 a.m. – 7 p.m.
Saturday + Sunday 10 a.m. – 7 p.m.

SUNDAY EXCURSIONS

Schlachtensee Lake – jogging, bathing and then the beer garden
Berlin is a genuine paradise for day-trippers. A string of fabulous lakes meanders in and around Berlin. This green city is blessed with an abundance of trees and parks. Berlin is perfect in the summertime. It's easy to access Schlachtensee Lake which is a particular attraction for joggers – one lap of the lake takes about half an hour.

Schlachtensee S-Bahn station is no more than 50 m away. In summer, you can go swimming, then order crispy chicken with potato

DO SOMETHING YOU HAVE NEVER DONE BEFORE

Badeschiff on the River Spree

Relax in all seasons by the River Spree on the Badeschiff. The floating pool was built by converting an old transport barge that is anchored as a swimming pool in the middle of Berlin's East harbour. This unique facility offers Berliners direct access to their river with a wonderful view over the Spree, Oberbaumbrücke and the television tower. The wooden boardwalk with sandy beach and beach bar is a popular place in summer with the fashionable crowd. At the end of a long day, everyone relaxes with a cocktail in hand and listens to pop music. During the winter months the Badeschiff is transformed into a into a covered, caterpillar-like island with sauna, pool and panoramic views.

Eichenstraße 4, Treptow
Phone: 0049 (0)152 059 45 752
www.badeschiff.de
May – September: Daily 8 a.m. – midnight
October – April: Monday, Tuesday, Thursday and Sunday noon – midnight, Friday and Saturday noon – 3 a.m. (Ladies only and men only sauna days can be found on the website)

salad from the beer garden at the Fischerhütte and eat under a shady tree with a lakeside view. The older main restaurant with its large fireplace serves traditional Austrian cuisine such as veal goulash, Tafelspitz (Austrian boiled beef) and Wiener Schnitzel.

Fischerhütte am Schlachtensee
Fischerhüttenstraße 136, Zehlendorf
Phone: 0049 (0)30 80498310
www.fischerhuette-berlin.de
Daily 9 a.m. – midnight

Potsdam

When in Berlin, a visit to Potsdam is almost a must – at least in summer. This cultural gem boasts attractions that would fill an entire book, but here are some tips for a successful day out in Potsdam. The easiest way to travel is by S-Bahn from Alexanderplatz via Berlin Zoo to Potsdam centre. We recommend hiring a bicycle, as it takes time to get around Potsdam on foot. Fortunately, there's a bike rental kiosk at Potsdam station. Now all you need is a map and you can set off! First, take a left turn onto Friedrich-Ebert-Straße towards Nauener Tor, where you can enjoy a break at Café Haider, or one of the other nearby cafés and watch life go by. The restored Dutch quarter with plenty of small shops and picturesque street scene begins right behind Nauener Tor. Next, head for Sanssouci Palace with its magnificent estate and parkland that extends as far as the Neuer Palais. Although cycling in the parks isn't strictly allowed, almost everybody does so and you usually reach your destination without any trouble. Cycle along Voltaireweg past the wooden houses in the Russian colony and on to Neuer Garten. Continue past the Marble Palace towards Cecilienhof Palace. A few metres further to the right is a spacious bathing park for those who need a refreshing dip. Otherwise, continue behind Cecilienhof Palace for five minutes longer until you reach the Meierei brewery and restaurant at Jungfernsee Lake. This lakeside location offers beautiful views and the microbrewery serves fresh beer with hearty Berlin beer garden food, including pork knuckle with classic pease pudding, pork sausages with beer and onion gravy and mashed potatoes. The light Prussian version would be potato with quark. In the colder weather you can eat inside the lovingly restored vaulted restaurant.

Meierei – Brauhaus
Im Neuen Garten 10, Potsdam
Tel: 0049 (0)331 7043211
www.meierei-potsdam.de
Winter (from the end of October):
Tuesday – Saturday noon – 10 p.m., Sunday to 8 p.m., summer (from April):
Tuesday–Sunday 11 a.m. – 10 p.m.

Heilandskirche
(Church of Our Saviour)
A worthwhile excursion is to Heilandskirche in Sacrow. This Italianate gem built in 1844 with its wonderfully tiled facades and graceful colonnade is located in Heilandspark directly on the Havel.

If you have the time, the bus ride to the church from Theodor-Heuss-Platz takes 60 minutes and from March to October you can take the Potsdam water taxi.

Sacrower Schlosspark
Fährstraße, Potsdam-Sacrow
www.heilandskirche-sacrow.de

www.potsdamer-wassertaxi.de

You should definitely break your return journey at HavelGut in Gatow. A large orange sign points downhill to a campsite where a young farmers' collective has taken over a restaurant. The wooden hut and garden evokes olde-worlde charm, but the menu is modern and innovative: wild boar burgers, water buffalo ham, Maultaschen (Swabian ravioli) filled with pumpkin and homemade cakes. All the food is served on old GDR crockery. There is also a stall selling organic vegetables. In the summer the barbecue is also fired up.

Kladower Damm 217, Gatow
www.speisegut.com
Wednesday – Sunday, 1 p.m. – 10 p.m.
(Please note that opening times are sometimes erratic – it's best to check first on www.facebook.com/HavelGut)

KREUZKÖLLN – THE BEST OF

'Kreuzkölln', between Kreuzberg and Neukölln, is Berlin's trendy district. Creative people from around the world live here and their interesting cafés and concept stores are constantly setting new trends.

Concierge.

The best coffee is served at Concierge. This charming boutique coffee shop is hidden away in a secluded rear courtyard at Paul-Lincke-Ufer. Photographer Namy Nosratifard and his partner Benjamin Pates supply the agencies and locals with the perfect cappuccino, flat white or apple tart – everything is handed through a small porter's hatch. The loyal customer base appreciates this personal touch.

At Cocolo next door you can try the delicious Japanese ramen soup with homemade noodles and various ingredients, rice tea, sake and matcha ice cream. In summer, you can sit outside on the pleasant terrace. On the other side of Landwehr Canal, Katies Blue Cat has a fabulous choice of shortbread with cranberry, Earl Grey or lavender, cookies, scones and cakes. A popular savoury snack is tasty sour dough bread with cheddar cheese and red onion and chilli chutney.

Sing Blackbird – a few hundred metres away at Sanderstraße – is the place to go for vegan pancakes, brown rice bowls and second-hand bargains. A flea market is also held every second Sunday of the month. Diana Durdic has even made it into the pages of Italian Vogue with her vegan café and vintage clothes.

At Melbourne Canteen several Australians serve the best selection from back home. You can spend the entire day at this white-tiled, light, spacious, cool café. At Two for Two, further along across the road, you'll find Japanese stationery and French patisserie. Apart from being attuned to the zeitgeist, two friends Eri and Tose are also baking gurus. They spoil their visitors with homemade madeleines, mini quiches, cannelés and matcha cookies.

Concierge Coffee
Paul-Lincke-Ufer 39-40, Kreuzberg
Monday – Friday 8:30 – 6 p.m., Saturday and Sunday 11 a.m. – 5 p.m.

Cocolo Ramen
Paul-Lincke-Ufer 39, Kreuzberg
Daily noon – 11 p.m.

Katies Blue Cat
Friedelstraße 31, Neukölln
www.katiesbluecat.de
Monday – Friday 8:30 a.m. – 8:30 p.m., Saturday and Sunday 10 a.m. – 7 p.m.

Sing Blackbird
Sanderstraße 11, Neukölln
Phone: 0049 (0)30 54845051
www.singblackbird.tumblr.com
Daily 11:30 a.m. – 8 p.m.

Melbourne Canteen
Pannierstr. 57, Neukölln
Phone: 0049 (0)30 62731602
www.melbournecanteen.com
Daily 9 a.m. – midnight

Two and Two
Pannierstr. 6
Berlin, Neukölln
www.twoandtwoberlin.com
Monday 8:30 a.m. – 6 p.m.,
Saturday and Sunday
10 a.m. – 6 p.m.

BOOKS TO READ

'Axolotl Roadkill' (2009),
by Helene Hegemann
Helene Hegemann's debut novel – published when she was just 18 – caused a furore. It recounts the story of a teenage dropout who lives between Berlin-Friedrichshain and Mitte. However, the fall from grace came when it was revealed that Hegemann plagiarized whole passages from the novel 'Strobo' by blogger Airen who described his wild nightlife at the Berghain nightclub. This is like two novels rolled into one – and an insight into Berlin's decadent side.

'Berlin Alexanderplatz' (1929),
by Alfred Döblin
Translation by Anne Thompson of Alfred Döblin's masterpiece set in 1920's Berlin towards the end of the jazz and music-hall era of the Roaring Twenties. Franz Biberkopf

is released after four years in prison for killing his girl-friend in a fit of rage. He makes a vow that he will go straight and lead a decent life, but his corrupt environment makes it impossible and despite all his efforts he is plunged step by step into the louche underworld of gangsters, prostitutes and pimps. Anne Thompson's translation captures the atmosphere of cosmopolitan Berlin towards the end of the Weimar Republic, and of the life of Berliners in the streets of the working-class area of Berlin around the Alexanderplatz square.

FILMS TO WATCH

'The Lives of Others' (Germany 2006)
Florian Henckel von Donnersmarck

Director Florian Henckel von Donnersmarck's Oscar-winning film is a drama about the Stasi, the GDR's secret police. In summer 1984, Stasi Captain Wiesler is instructed to spy on the playwright Georg Dreyman and his girlfriend Christa-Maria. This changes the lives of all three and gives an insight into East Berlin's cultural scene and realities in the GDR. One of the film's last scenes is set in the legendary Karl Marx bookshop at Karl-Marx-Allee, now the head offices of several agencies..

'The Blue Angel' (Germany 1930)
Josef von Sternberg

For director Josef von Sternberg and Marlene Dietrich it all began with The Blue Angel, one of the masterpieces of Germany's Weimar cinema. This landmark film thrust the sultry and unrestrained Dietrich on an unsuspecting international film audience. She plays the prototypical role of Lola, the singer who tempts repressed professor Emil Jannings into complete submission night after night at the Blue Angel night-club. The film perfectly captures the masochism and degradation of the Weimar Republic, just before the rise of Adolf Hitler.

PERSONALITIES

Michael Ballhaus (born 1935)
As a cinematographer, Michael Ballhaus is one of the leading figures of German and international film. His work pioneered New German Film in the 1970s. He shot seventeen films with Rainer Werner Fassbinder alone – making him famous in the film world outside Germany, and opening doors in Hollywood. His films have been nominated for several Oscars.

Heinz Berggruen (1914 – 2007)
Berggruen was one of the leading German art collectors of the 20th century; he was a journalist, writer, art dealer, gallerist and patron. Sixty years after his emigration in 1936, he returned to Berlin and bequeathed his valuable collection of paintings to his native city for a modest amount. The collection of 113 great contemporary artists is currently on display at the Stülerbau, the Museum Berggruen opposite Charlottenburg Palace.

Helmut Newton (1920 – 2004)
One of the best, most controversial and expensive photographers in the world hails from Berlin. His erotic style revolutionized fashion photography.

IMPORTANT INFORMATION

Tourist information office:
Berlin Info Store
in the Hauptbahnhof, ground floor/
Entrance Europaplatz, Tiergarten
Daily 8 a.m. – 10 p.m.
www.berlin-tourist-information.de

Telephone dialling codes:
Germany: 0049
Berlin: (0)30

Airports:
Berlin-Tegel
Taxi to the city centre: approximately 25 minutes/about €20
Airport bus TXL to Berlin central station: approximately
20 minutes/€2.60
Airport bus TXL to Alexanderplatz: approximately 25 mins./€2.60
Airport bus X9 to Zoologischer Garten station: approximately
20 mins./€2.60

Berlin-Schönefeld
Taxi to the city centre: approximately 45 minutes/about €35
Airport Express to central station: approximately 30 mins./about €3.20

Radio Taxis:
Würfelfunk: 0049 (0)30 210101
Taxifunk: 0049 (0)30 443322

Bicycle rental:
Fahrradstation
Hotline: 0180 5108000
www.fahrradstation.de

City magazines:
Zitty and Tip (biweekly, in rotation)

MY PERFECT WEEKEND

Friday:
___
___
___
___
___
___

Saturday:
___
___
___
___
___
___

Sunday:
___
___
___
___
___
___

NOTES